MONEY AND THE CHURCH

MONEY
and
the
CHURCH

by *LUTHER P. POWELL*

ASSOCIATION PRESS ∿ NEW YORK

Preface

When I earned my first dollar at the age of 12 years, my mother explained to me the principle of tithing. This was the beginning of my interest in Christian stewardship. As I, the son of a Methodist minister, grew older, I became increasingly aware of the discrepancy between the Good News which the church proclaimed and the rather careless and miserly way in which Christians supported the gospel financially. Although I felt this discrepancy primarily because of the financial hardships which we in the manse had to endure, yet there was awakened in me a desire to see this inconsistency reconciled.

While I was in college, I accepted God's call to the Christian ministry, and for three years served two small rural churches as a college student supply pastor. The Lord's Acre movement was receiving considerable publicity, and I introduced this plan to my people. During those years, however, the grain seed died in the ground because of lack of rain.

After completing my B.D. work in seminary, I was encouraged by Dr. Ralph A. Felton to investigate further the problem of financial support in the rural church. This study culminated in an M.A. thesis entitled "A study of financial support as it relates to the present decline in the number of ministers, with special emphasis upon the rural church."

Yet, my question about the lack of harmony between the gospel and its support was not answered. Therefore, I continued my studies in the area of church support, turning more to the past records as they threw light on the motives and methods of giving. Out of this search came the Ph.D. thesis, submitted to Drew Theological Seminary in 1951, entitled: "The Growth and Development of the Motives and Methods of Church Support with Special Emphasis Upon the American Churches."

For the past ten years I have continued to search for further insights into the motives and methods of giving, and this book is the result of my inquiry which actually began at the age of 12 years when I was instructed in the principle of tithing.

It would be impossible to acknowledge all the help I have received from individuals and libraries in the quest for this information. However, I do want to express my gratitude to three individuals: Dr. Ralph A. Felton, of Drew Theological Seminary, who would not let me rest until every possible resource had been exhausted; Rev. Thomas K. Thompson, Executive Director of the Department of Stewardship and Benevolence of the National Council of the Churches of Christ in the U.S.A., whose dedication to Christian Stewardship has helped tremendously to bring this work to publication; and to Rev. Richard L. Peterman, Associate Director of the Stewardship Department and Lutheran Laymen's Movement of the United Lutheran Church in America, for his capable assistance in preparing the manuscript for publication.

LUTHER P. POWELL

Contents

Preface 5

Introduction 11

PART ONE—MONEY AND THE CHURCH PREVIOUS TO THE
AMERICAN PERIOD

I. The Early Church to Constantine 15
Voluntary offerings
First fruits
Tithing
Endowments

II. Constantine to Gregory the Great 25
Endowments and legacies
Oblations
First fruits
Tithing
Decrees of councils on the tithe

III. The Middle Ages (Methods) 32
Gifts
Vacancies
Papal taxations
Church courts

IV. The Middle Ages (Motives) 53
Revenue-producing doctrines
Indulgences

Relics

Absolutions and dispensations

V. The Reformation and Later in Europe . . .   66

The tithe system

Church rates

State support

PART TWO—MONEY AND THE CHURCH IN EARLY AMERICA

VI. Philosophies of Voluntary Support   85

On the congregational level

On the national level

VII. Philosophies of Compulsory Support . . .   104

On the town level

By the authority of the patroon

By the authority of the colony and the king

VIII. Methods of Support   123

Glebes

Pew revenues

Collections and offerings

Subscription lists

Lotteries

PART THREE—MONEY AND THE CHURCH IN CONTEMPORARY AMERICA

IX. Lottery and Merchandising   151

Variations of the lottery

Bingo

Merchandising schemes

Church farm and Lord's Acre

Business enterprises

Activity and faith

X. Every Member Canvass 173
  Budgets
  Education and promotion
  Pledges
  Envelopes
  Youth participation
  Secondary accomplishments
  Professional fund raisers

XI. Motives for Giving 183
  Oblation and fear
  Legal compulsion
  Personal glorification
  Personal profit
  Self-interest
  Missionary
  Love

XII. Guiding Principles 201
  Stewardship
  Proportionate giving
  First fruits

XIII. The Discipline of Tithing 213
  A rise in interest
  Tithing defined
  Five witnesses for tithing

XIV. The Ministry of Christian Giving 229
  The gospel imperative
  The meaning of money
  Money is you
  Evangelists all

  Notes by Chapters 237

Introduction

Money has always played an important role in the Christian church.

The twelve men whom Jesus called to be his disciples selected one of their number to handle the money required for their material needs. From that first small group to the present day the church has found it necessary to obtain money for her program. However, a great variety of motives and methods have been used by the church to acquire this money. The purpose of this book is twofold: first, to trace the various motives and methods throughout the history of the Christian church and to examine them in the light of history, the Bible, and the highest standards of our time; and, second, to attempt to set forth some guiding principles for financing the church today.

The importance of this study is sustained at two points. First, it is in the realm of financial support that the church has been most vulnerable. In seeking support she has been tempted constantly to exploit and abuse the very things for which she stands. Although reforms have taken place in the church, financial support continues to be a point in her program at which she is apt to stumble. In the second place, the importance of this study rests on the fact that the outreach of the church today, as in the past, depends to a great extent on material means, and unless these means are adequately met, the "Great Commission" of Christ, "Go into all the world" will not be realized in this or future generations.

History is like a cord which is made up of many strands. In studying any subject historically, one might separate the strands and examine them individually. Or, one might take all the strands or events in a given period and examine them in their relation to one another. The former approach emphasizes a topical structure while the latter makes chronology predominant.

In the following pages the motives and methods in church support are discussed both topically and chronologically. In this way the reader can see the growth and development of a particular method both within a specific period in the history of the church and within the entire history of the church. An attempt also has been made to show patterns which recur. For instance, the conflict between the principle of voluntary allegiance and methods of compulsory support can be traced throughout most of the church's history. Also, the practice of simony—exchanging spiritual things for money—shows itself from time to time under various forms. Another kind of pattern is seen when one observes the relation between certain kinds of theology and the motives and methods of finance which are supported by the theological concepts.

It is hoped that out of this endeavor certain principles can be drawn which might spare the church from pitfalls which she has experienced in the past. More positively it is hoped that these guiding principles may enlighten the financial activities of the church in the present day as well as in the future.

part **ONE**

MONEY AND THE CHURCH
PREVIOUS TO THE
AMERICAN PERIOD

I. The Early Church to Constantine
     Voluntary offerings
     First fruits
     Tithing
     Endowments

II. Constantine to Gregory the Great
     Endowments and legacies
     Oblations
     First fruits
     Tithing
     Decrees of councils on the tithe

III. The Middle Ages (Methods)
     Gifts
     Vacancies
     Papal taxations
     Church courts

IV. The Middle Ages (Motives)
     Revenue-producing doctrines
     Indulgences
     Relics
     Absolutions and dispensations

V. The Reformation and Later in Europe
     The tithe system
     Church rates
     State support

I

The Early Church
to Constantine

The Christian church of the first three centuries received money in four ways: (1) through voluntary offerings—that is, a gift of money or in kind to support the church in its charitable, missionary, or other activities; (2) through the giving of first fruits; (3) through the giving of tithes; and (4) through endowments.

In the first century of the church, three claims of support were made on the congregations: (1) the relief of the sick and poor; (2) the support of apostles and other traveling missionaries; and (3) the expenses connected with the public meetings. The first two of these claims provided the beginnings of financial support in the church.

Voluntary Offerings

A serious financial crisis developed in Jerusalem within a very short time following the resurrection and ascension of our Lord. Believers had come into Jerusalem to join the fellowship, and in time their funds were exhausted. Those who had property were moved to sell some of it and bring it into the common treasury.* 1

The faithful believed Christ's return was not far off, and many

* All numbered notes will be found under "Notes by Chapters" at the end of the book.

had abandoned their trades or avocations, losing their sources of income. Luke's account implies they were living on their capital. Thus, the church at Jerusalem was soon threatened by poverty.

At first, no evidence is given of any central controlling authority. However, as the work grew in size, more organization was necessary. Thus, the Seven [2] were appointed to handle this work. In other words, the financial crisis in Jerusalem compelled the early church to provide for a commission on finance. Prior to Paul's directives in First and Second Corinthians there was probably no permanent financial organization. Referring to his instructions at a previous time, Paul wrote to the Corinthians: "As I have given order to the churches of Galatia, even so do ye. Upon the first day of the week let every one of you lay by him in store as God hath prospered him." [3] Paul ignored any common treasury, directing each to keep his own money.

Undoubtedly, the collection for the poor of Jerusalem established the precedent of accumulating a sum of money toward which all contributed and over which the church appointed trustees.[4]

Although the financial arrangements for the poor and sick may have developed differently in the various churches, eventually there was a move to make permanent provision in the churches to care for the needy. For example, in I Timothy, Paul urges that as far as possible relatives were to care for the widows so that the church could take care of those who were without families, those who were "widows indeed." It is evident that these were funds belonging to the whole body.

The second claim, placed on the congregation, was for the support of apostles and other traveling missionaries. Respecting their maintenance, our Lord had indicated the principle: "The laborer is worthy of his hire." [5] The same principle is laid down by Paul and illustrated by several similitudes—the soldier drawing his pay, the vine-dresser reaping the fruit of his vineyard, the shepherd living on the milk of his flock, and the ox being free to feed while treading out the corn.[6] Paul leaves no doubt as to the interpretation of the similitudes, for he states: "Even so hath the Lord ordained that they which preach the gospel should live of the gospel." [7] When he writes to Timothy [8] concerning the elders being counted worthy of double honor, the idea of remuneration is included, and he states that as the ox is not muzzled while treading out corn, so the laborer is worthy of his reward.

Although Paul himself did not receive compensation from the church at Corinth, he did receive financial aid from the faithful of Philippi. Even though he had learned to face plenty and hunger, abundance and want, he was grateful for the Philippian aid. In fact, he stated it had been they alone who had provided for his needs.[9] And, although Paul was determined not to burden the Corinthians, he did let them know he had been enabled to serve them because of the gifts of other churches.[10]

From the few records still in existence, it appears that people gave with a benevolent spirit. Paul reminded the Corinthians of the generosity of the churches of Macedonia and directed them to respond remembering the "grace of our Lord Jesus Christ, that, though he was rich, yet for your sakes he became poor, that ye through his poverty might be rich." [11]

Did this motivation prevail? Comments of Paul would lead us to believe that it did, and that his parishioners were generous.

Three writings which appeared in the second century show generosity was practiced. The first, the *Apology of Aristides,* written to the Emperor Hadrian about A.D. 135 reveals unusual benevolence:

> And if there is among them a man that is poor or
> needy, and they have not an abundance of neces-
> saries, they fast two or three days that they may
> supply the needy with their necessary food.[12]

Also, Justin Martyr spoke of the custom of giving as it was being practiced in Samaria in A.D. 140:

> And the wealthy among us help the needy. . . .
> And they who are well to do, and willing, give
> what each thinks fit; and what is collected is
> deposited with the president, who succours the
> orphans and widows, and those who, through
> sickness or any other cause, are in want, and
> those who are in bonds, and the strangers
> sojourning among us, and in a word takes care
> of all who are in need.[13]

Tertullian at Carthage, A.D. 199, inviting the rulers of the Roman world to examine the practice of the Christians, reported they made voluntary monthly offerings for the church and the needy. The gifts were entirely voluntary, and the motive unselfish.

> Though we have our treasure-chest, it is not made
> up of purchase-money, as of a religion that has
> its price. On the monthly collection day, if he
> likes, each puts in a small donation; but only if it
> be his pleasure, and only if he is able; for there is
> no compulsion; all is voluntary. These gifts are, as
> it were, piety's deposit fund. For they are not
> taken thence and spent on feasts, and drinking-
> bouts, and eating-houses, but to support and bury
> poor people, to supply the wants of boys and
> girls destitute of means and parents, and of old
> persons confined now to the house; such, too, as
> have suffered shipwreck; and if there happens to
> be any in the mines, or banished to the islands,
> or shut up in the prisons, for nothing but their
> fidelity to the cause of God's church, they become
> the nurslings of their confession.[14]

That is motivation of a high caliber.

First Fruits

Although neither the amount nor the proportion was defined, first fruits were given by the Christians of the first three or four centuries. First fruits are urged in the *Didache* as follows:

> But every true prophet desiring to settle among
> you is worthy of his food. In like manner, a true
> teacher is also worthy, like the workman, of his
> food. Every first-fruit, then, of the produce of
> the wine-vat and of the threshing-floor, of thy
> oxen and of thy sheep, thou shalt take and give as
> the first-fruit to the prophets; for they are your
> chief priests. But if ye have not a prophet, give
> them to the poor. If thou makest bread, take the
> first-fruit and give according to the commandment.
> In like manner, when thou openest a jar of wine,
> or oil, take the first-fruit and give to the prophets;
> yea, and of money and raiment and every posses-
> sion take the first-fruit, as shall seem good to thee,
> and give according to the commandment.[15]

In each case the amount is left up to the individual. It is also significant that the *Didache* calls for first fruits on the basis of principle, not because of a specific need.

Irenaeus, believing Christ had set the example of first fruits when he took bread and wine at the Last Supper, urged the giving of such fruits: "We are bound, therefore, to offer to God the first fruits of His creation." [16] However, this, of course, is an accommodation of the Last Supper to the argument in question.

The Apostolical Constitutions, a work which may not have been completed until the fourth century, but surely reflects the teaching of the period that preceded the actual writing, makes the following requirement concerning first fruits:

> All the first-fruits of the wine-press, the threshing-
> floor, the oxen, and the sheep, shalt thou give to

the priests, that thy store-houses and garners and
the products of thy land may be blessed, and
thou mayest be strengthened with corn and wine
and oil, and the herds of thy cattle and flocks of
thy sheep may be increased. Thou shalt give the
tenth of thy increase to the orphans, and to the
widow, and to the poor, and to the stranger. All the
first-fruits of thy hot bread, of thy barrels of wine,
or oil, or honey, or nuts, or grapes, or the first-
fruits of other things, shalt thou give to the priests;
but those of silver, and of garments, and of all sort
of possessions, to the orphan and to the widow.[17]

Origen has an important passage on first fruits in his eleventh
homily on Numbers XVIII:

It is fit and profitable that first fruits be offered to
(or "for") the priests of the gospel also, for so also
hath the Lord ordained, that they who preach the
gospel should live of the gospel, and that those
who wait at the altar should participate from the
altar. And as this is worthy and decent, so, on the
contrary, I think it indecent, unworthy, and
impious, that he who worships God, and enters
the house of God, who knows that priests and
ministers wait at the altar, and serve either to the
(preaching of) the word or to the ministry of the
church, should not offer to the priests the first
fruits of the fruits of the earth which God gives by
making the sun to shine and the rain to fall. Such
a soul seems to me to have no remembrance of
God, nor to think, nor to believe He gave the fruits
which he has received, since he hoards them up
as if God had nothing to do with them; for, if he
believed them to have been given to him by God,
he would know how to honour God by rewarding
the priests out of his gifts and rewards.[18]

There can be no doubt that the Christians of the first three
centuries were instructed to give first fruits to the church. How-

ever, a specific amount for the first fruits was not indicated; instead, each person was encouraged to give out of gratitude for the gifts of creation and redemption.

Tithing

In the first century of the Christian church there is little evidence that tithing was recommended for Christians. Jesus spoke of tithes or tithing only twice—in the parable of the Pharisee and the Publican [19] and in the denunciation of the Pharisees.[20]

The absence of any reaffirmation of the principle of the tithe in the New Testament does not decide the case either for or against tithing as a broad principle of stewardship. The absence does, however, fail to give satisfactory evidence that tithes were paid by first-century Christians.

When the collection was made for the poor in Jerusalem, each gave "according to his ability," [21] and in the churches of Galatia and Corinth, each is directed to give "as God hath prospered him." [22] Also, in the epistle to Timothy (where Paul speaks of the finances of the church) there is no mention of tithes or of any other fixed proportion.

The tithe is mentioned occasionally in the second century, but the emphasis is upon the fact that Christians, living under grace, will not be limited by a tithe. The general testimony of the writers is that the generosity of the Christians went farther than a mere tenth.

A case in point is Irenaeus (A.D. 120-202) who contrasted the Jewish law with the teachings of Jesus and showed that Jesus fulfilled and extended the law:

> ... and instead of the law enjoining the giving
> of tithes, [He told us] to share all our possessions
> with the poor; and not to love our neighbours
> only, but even our enemies; and not merely to be
> liberal givers and bestowers, but even that we

should present a gratuitous gift to those who take
away our goods.[23]

Irenaeus goes on to point out that the difference between the
conditions of the law and the teaching of Jesus is that the offering now is made "not by slaves, but by freemen." Then he con-
trasts what should be the giving of the Christians with the limi-
tation of the tithe. Also, in contrasting the law-centered motive
of the Jews with the motive of the Christians, Irenaeus states
that "those who have received liberty" and "have the hope of
better things," will not give less than the tithe, but will "set aside
all their possessions for the Lord's purposes." [24]

The tithe as a standard of giving was supported in the third
century. Origen, in his eleventh Homily on Numbers XVIII,
argues that Luke 11:42 teaches that although the Lord would
have the greater things of the law done, he would not have the
other things—such as tithing—left undone. To those who would
have excused themselves from tithing on the basis that Jesus
was not speaking to his disciples, but to Pharisees, Origen
quoted Matthew 5:20, "Except your righteousness exceed that
of scribes and Pharisees, ye shall not enter into the kingdom
of heaven."

The paragraph from *The Apostolical Constitutions,* previously quoted, contains one sentence which mentions the tithe.
It reads, "Thou shalt give the tenth of thy increase to the
orphans, and to the widow, and to the poor, and to the stranger." Here is evidence that the faithful were being urged to give
a tenth "of the increase" to the needy as well as the first fruits
to the clergy.

Other excerpts from *The Apostolical Constitutions* make
strong implications that the ministers are in a role similar to
that of the Levites. Also, the *Constitutions* reminds the people
that even though they have been delivered from the additional

bonds of sacrificing creatures for sin offerings, purifications, scapegoats, and continual washings and sprinklings, nevertheless, Jesus "has nowhere freed you from those oblations which you owe to the priest, nor from doing good to the poor." [25]

Cyprian (A.D. 200-258) refers to tithing, but he does not urge it as a Christian practice. This absence of instruction on tithing in the writings of Cyprian is significant. In his treatise on Works and Alms, Cyprian went to extreme lengths to accommodate Scripture to support the practice of almsgiving, but he completely ignores the wealth of Old Testament material on tithing. His only mention of tithing was to contrast the practice of giving a tenth with the lack of generosity of which some Christians were guilty.[26]

The fact that these early Christian writers did not stress first fruits and tithes as they did almsgiving is worthy of consideration. Some were very bold in accommodating Old Testament principles to Christian faith and practice. This was true especially in the relation between almsgiving and righteousness. Paul's thesis of the righteousness of Christ was ignored almost completely as many writers upheld the righteousness of almsgiving.

Yet, these same writers avoided the snare of substituting the law of the tithe for the voluntary principle of giving. Reference was made to the law of the tithe, but with few exceptions it was added that giving for the Christian was no longer dependent upon this taskmaster.

Endowments

The first three centuries of the church introduced a means of finance that was to be one of her chief sources of revenue throughout the coming centuries, namely, endowments.

Previous to Maximum and the relief which he, Constantine, and Licinius gave to the church, real estate which was endowed to the church was in constant danger of being confiscated by the emperors. Therefore, most immovable endowment property was sold, and the money received was divided into three equal parts: one part to the church, one to the bishop, and one to the rest of the clergy.[27]

However, not all endowed property was sold. As early as the year A.D. 200 some Christian communities kept within the law by owning burial grounds. Also, from the fact that later decrees ordered a restoration of confiscated property, it is certain the Christian communities held property as a corporate body during this early period.

In 313, Maximum, returning from defeat, denounced the gods he had honored previously and issued an order for the restoration of the property of the Christian church. That same year Constantine and Licinius also published a decree directing that all confiscated property of the Christians be returned. In this order permission was granted to the Christians to build the "Lord's houses." [28]

In summary, it is possible to conclude that the early Christians —in the main—were motivated in their giving by a compassion to relieve suffering and to extend the gospel to the world. This motivation resulted in giving procedures that stand out as a beacon in the history of giving in the Christian church.

II

Constantine to Gregory the Great

Following the Edict of Milan, Constantine showed increasing favor toward the Christians. This favor encouraged growth in the church—growth in numbers of persons and in program; consequently, it led to more intricate financial activities.

Endowments and Legacies

In A.D. 321 Constantine opened the way for the church to receive legacies by ruling that "everyone has permission to leave when he is dying whatsoever goods he wishes to the most holy Catholic Church. . . ." [1]

The growing belief that gifts would aid in the ransom of their souls encouraged many Christians to endow the church liberally. Many bequeathed all their property to the church, leaving in poverty those dependent upon them. Thus, measures were taken to protect the people from destitution by controlling these legacies. Laws were written to stop unscrupulous priests who attempted to induce people to will their estates to them personally. Jerome and Ambrose did not object to these laws, but they did lament the fact that such laws were considered necessary.

Oblations

The term oblation was coming into prominence during this period. It denotes a particular spirit in which a gift is given. It generally indicates a motive rather than a method, the motive being to acquire salvation. It became one of the most important means by which the church was supported in later years, particularly in the Middle Ages.

Originally, the term oblation referred to the elements of bread and wine which were brought by the worshipers and presented at the altar as a sacrifice. The Council of Mascon (A.D. 585) decreed "that on every Lord's Day an oblation of the altar should be offered by all, men and women, both bread and wine." [2] But, it was not long until oblations were not confined to bread and wine. Gifts in money and in kind were being presented at the altar, and it became more and more difficult to draw the line between oblations and offerings.

The motive for the giving was not primarily to support the church in its material need, nor was it to provide a ministry for others; rather, it was to acquire salvation for the donor and his family. This motive can be seen in many accounts of giving. Examples need not be given at this point, for the oblation motive shows itself in a number of methods which will be discussed later. The oblation motive is carried to its ultimate conclusion in the revenue-producing doctrine.

First Fruits

Little emphasis is placed on first fruits as a method of supporting the church in this period. It was, of course, mentioned from time to time but was losing its appeal as a practical procedure.

It is impossible to ascertain just how the term was used in the few usages of it after the fourth century.

Tithing

As we proceed beyond the fourth century we find a growing emphasis on tithing until it becomes, first, a law of the church, and, finally, a law of the civil courts.

The sermons and exhortations of some of the leading theologians of the period had a considerable influence in helping to develop tithing as a primary method of church support.

In his letter to Nepotain, Jerome (A.D. 345-420) stated he was in the heritage of the Lord, and like the priest and the Levite, "I live on the tithe, and serving the altar, am supported by its offering." [3] In his exhortation on Malachi 3:10, Jerome states that if we are not willing to sell all and give to the poor and follow the Lord, the least we can do is to imitate the rudimentary teachings of the Jews, and, if one fails to do this much, "he is convicted of defrauding and cheating God." [4] Even though the tithe is not mentioned, the implication of Jerome's admonition is quite clear—the "teachings of the Jews" which the Christians were to imitate was the giving of tithes.

Ambrose of Milan (A.D. 340-397) leaves no doubt as to his message to Christians on tithing.

> God has reserved the tenth part to Himself, and
> therefore it is not lawful for a man to retain what
> God had reserved for Himself. To thee He has
> given nine parts, for Himself He has reserved the
> tenth part, and if thou shalt not give to God the
> tenth part, God will take from thee the nine parts.[5]

In an Ascension Day sermon, Ambrose declares, "A good Christian pays tithes yearly to be given to the poor." [6] He urges tithing in other sermons, too, but in Sermon 34, by distorting the meaning of the parable of the talents, he draws a conclusion which influenced succeeding preachers:

> That of all the substance which God hath given us,
> He hath reserved a Tenth part to Himself; that
> therefore it is not lawful to retain that which God
> hath reserved to Himself. That God will take away
> the nine parts if we do not give him the tenth, and

> that he who doth not restore what he hath sub-
> tracted of those Tithes neither fears God nor
> knows what true repentance meaneth.[7]

Augustine (A.D. 354-430) contributed additional material in support of the tithe in his sermons and comments on the Scriptures. Discussing Psalm 147, he declared the laborer is worthy of his hire, and he urged a proportionate gift and suggested a tenth was little enough. His discussion shows the kind of reasoning being used to support the tithe.

> Cut off some part of thy income; a tenth if thou
> choosest, though that is but little. For it is said that
> the Pharisees gave a tenth; "I fast twice in the
> week, I give tithes of all that I possess" (Luke
> 18:12). And what saith the Lord? "Except your
> righteousness exceed the righteousness of the
> scribes and Pharisees, ye shall not enter into the
> kingdom of heaven" (Matthew 5:20). He whose
> righteousness thou oughtest to exceed, gives a
> tenth; thou givest not even a thousandth. How wilt
> thou surpass him whom thou matchest not? [8]

This is clearly an accommodation of Scripture to support tithing. In his Homily XLVIII, Augustine contends their ancestors used to abound in wealth because they gave tithes, but now, because devotion to God has ceased, the treasury has been drained. Then, like Ambrose, he claims, "We have been unwilling to share the tithes with God, now the whole is taken away." [9]

In another sermon Augustine clearly pressed the payment of tithes, if one wished either pardon or reward:

> God, the giver of all, requires back a tenth part
> from us; that He requires Tithes of whatever is our
> livelihood; and that they are due as a debt; and
> that whosoever would procure of God either
> pardon or reward, must pay for them, and out of
> the nine parts remaining endeavor to give alms.[10]

Chrysostom, like Augustine, accommodates the Scripture in such a way as to make the tithe a minimum gift. He has a lengthy discussion of the tithe in Homily LXIV on Matthew. First, he states that except one's righteousness shall exceed that of the scribes and Pharisees, one shall not enter the kingdom of Heaven. Then he says, "So that though thou give alms, but not more than they, thou shalt not enter in." Following this statement he lists the kinds of giving of the faithful scribe or Pharisee, and estimates the total gift to be equal to at least three-tenths, and possibly as much as one-half.

> But if he who gave the third part of his goods, or
> rather the half, if then he who is giving the half,
> achieves no great thing, he who doth not bestow so
> much as the tenth, of what shall he be worthy?
> With reason He said, "There are few that be
> saved." [11]

In his Homily LXXIII, on Matthew 23:23, he lays great stress on the words of Jesus, "These ought ye to have done, and not leave the others undone." [12]

Priests used the Confessional to promote tithing. John Seldon gives a quotation from a *Penitential,* used by the priests in the Confessional. The date of this document cannot be set exactly, but it does give some idea of methods used to induce people to tithe. The quotation indicates that God accepted Abel's gift and rejected Cain's because Abel was honest in his tithing; Cain was dishonest in his. Thus, the first murder was committed because a dishonest tither was jealous of an honest tither.[13]

Thus we have seen the trend in the instruction on the tithe. At first, tithing was mentioned merely as a record of what was practiced by the Jews. Emphasis was placed on generosity on the part of the Christian, thus surpassing the tithe. The generosity of the people decreased, however, and apparently it became necessary—or expedient—to make a case for tithing from

Scripture. The case was made by appropriating Scripture; and the writings of Jerome, Ambrose, Augustine, and Chrystostom became the basis for promoting tithing throughout the church.

Decrees of Councils on the Tithe

The scriptural basis of tithing having been established, the next step was to give the tithe the support of church councils.

The earliest-known statement by a church council concerning tithes is one which appeared in a Circular Epistle, A.D. 567, in which the provincial Council of Tours directed people to make their due payment of tithes.[14]

Eighteen years later, A.D. 585, the second Council of Mascon made a canon respecting the payment of tithes. After reviewing former practices in the church this canon states:

> Wherefore we do appoint and decree, that the
> ancient custom be revived among the faithful, and
> that all the people bring in their Tithes to those
> who attend the Divine offices of the Church. If any
> one shall be contumacious to these our most
> wholesome orders, let him be forever separated
> from the Communion of the Church.[15]

If this is authentic, the most important line is the last, whereby the threat of excommunication is set before the people if they fail to tithe.

Five years later, A.D. 590, a similar canon was made by a Council held at Seville for the Kingdom of Spain, and it read:

> Tithes of all cattle, fruits, and labour of men, and
> decree him who should subtract any of these Tithes,
> to be a robber of God, and a thief, and that the
> curse which God inflicted upon Cain who did not
> divide aright unto God His portion be heaped
> upon him.[16]

By this time, the church was becoming large in numbers and moderately wealthy. Through the influence of various bishops of this period the papacy became very great. In A.D. 494 Pope Gelasius could write with confidence to the Eastern Emperor Anastasius and declare that of the two powers ruling the world —the pontiffs and the royal powers—the importance of the priests was much greater.[17]

Gregory the Great, who became pope in A.D. 590, greatly consolidated the power of the papacy. Thus it is Gregory who stands at a place in the history of the church which gives him prominence—standing at midstream, between a struggling, aspiring church and a powerful, commanding church.

III

The Middle Ages
(Methods)

It was under Gregory the Great that the papacy assumed the position of final authority over the church. Thus it is with him that a study of giving in the Middle Ages must begin.

Gregory was an energetic but kindly landlord, and he employed the income from the church's estates—which were becoming quite numerous—for the maintenance of the clergy, public worship, the defense of Rome, and in charitable foundations and good works of all kinds.[1]

Documents of the sixth century mention for the first time a papal *arcarius* (minister of finance). In the seventh century, reference is made to a papal administrator bearing the title *saccellarius,* whose duty it was to pay the soldiers and give alms to Rome.[2]

By A.D. 1017 the treasury department of the papal court was being designated as the "camera" or "chamber." The *camerarius,* a comparatively new official in the camera, kept the treasure.

The camera, or papal treasury, was established at the time when the popes were expanding politically and ecclesiastically and were outgrowing their incomes. The financial difficulties of the Apostolic See were becoming apparent in the time of Alexander III (1159-1181) who was forced to contract many loans. The existing sources of income were exhausted, and new taxes were sought.

By the beginning of the thirteenth century it was apparent that the constantly increasing needs of the papacy could not be met merely by a more rigid and orderly enforcement of payment of the old papal dues. Thus the popes began to seek new sources of income, and some of their methods defeated the purpose for which the papacy had been created.

The several methods by which the church of the Middle Ages was supported can be catalogued under these headings: (1) gifts, (2) vacancies, (3) papal taxations, and (4) church courts. This grouping, in a sense, is arbitrary, since some of the methods could be discussed under more than one heading.

In evaluating these financial transactions, it is well to remember that some methods grew out of medieval theology, others out of the accepted standards of the times, and still others out of the human weaknesses and appetites of individual leaders. Also, it must be remembered that the church and the clergy went no further than the traffic would bear; and this has been true, generally, of the efforts of the church to support herself throughout her history, even to the present day!

Gifts

There were a number of gifts that were presented for the support of the papacy. Though they do not fall into specific groups, a reasonable division might be as follows: (1) legacies, (2) subsidies, (3) tribute, and (4) gifts.

Legacies. From before the time of Gregory the Great, the church had received a considerable amount of property from legacies, made by the faithful. Throughout the Middle Ages, legacies continued to be given to the church. Some were recorded in the cameral registers; others went directly to the pope without passing through the camera.

Subsidies. These were gifts that were requested by the popes. They were used to meet various needs of the Apostolic See.

In A.D. 1093, Urban II called upon the bishops and abbots of Aquitaine, Gascony, and Lower Burgundy to request and gather subsidies to aid in the restoration of the liberty of the Apostolic See.[3] In later years the popes sent out agents to solicit gifts for the papacy. In 1251 the clergy of the province of Canterbury voluntarily offered to the pope a subsidy.

Subsidies, like some of the other sources of income, soon lost their voluntary character. The requests for aid became demands. To wit, in 1262 a papal mandate required the English prelates to pay a subsidy to the pope on the basis that the Roman Church, by divine institution, had undertaken burdens of expense for the defense of ecclesiastical liberty. And, in 1298, a similar request was sent to the prelates of France.

Apparently, a considerable amount of income was realized through these subsidies.

Tribute. The difference between tribute, census, and tax is not always clear. The tribute was a payment or "gift," which temporal rulers sent to the Apostolic See in return for protection. Sometimes the lay lord surrendered his lands into the hands of the pope and then received back the use of them. Thus, in case of invasion or attack, the papacy furnished the protection.

One of the earliest payments of tribute was undertaken by the first Christian duke of Poland near the close of the tenth century.[4] During the next century, several lay lords contracted to pay an annual sum to the papacy in return for protection. The best-known example is that promised by King John of England in 1213, who agreed to pay annually 1,000 marks of sterling.[5]

Oblations. The voluntary offerings made at the altars in Rome constituted one of the oldest sources of papal income. As early as 1356 these offerings were being shared with the clergy who took part in the services. Since they were oblations, the primary motive for these gifts was the donor's spiritual welfare.

Upon examination of the various gifts, it appears doubtful

whether all were "gifts" in the true sense of the word. If they were gifts, the motives were not always commendable. Although some gifts may have been given with no conditions attached, they generally carried a stated or implied proviso. Also, succeeding lords or kings did not always fulfill the commitments of their predecessors. Thus, compulsion of various forms had to be employed to collect the "gifts."

Vacancies

There were a number of ways in which vacant benefices called for financial transactions. If death had terminated the ministry of the previous bishop, the question arose as to whom his personal goods were to go. Also, there was the question of what was to be done with the income from the benefice during the interim.

Likewise, financial consideration soon entered into the appointments of the clergy to benefices. The financial transactions centering around vacancies came under the control of the papacy. These transactions fall under the following: (1) the spoils, (2) fruits during vacancy, (3) annates, (4) expectations, (5) illegitimate fruits, (6) services, (7) pallium, and (8) pluralities.

The Spoils. The "spoils" refers to the personal property of a clergyman at the time of his death. Almost from the first, various parties sought to claim this property. The church frequently attempted to guard against abuses in this matter by writing protective canons. Accordingly, the Council of Chalcedon, A.D. 451, ruled: "That it is not lawful for clergymen after the death of their bishop to seize what belongs to him, as has been forbidden by the canons of old time." [6]

In A.D. 524, a canon was written which directed that upon the death of a bishop, both clerics and relatives of the bishop were to keep "rapacious hands from all his property until they had the sanction either of the metropolitan bishop or four provincial bishops." [7]

Apparently, the canons did not check the abuse. Nobles and kings attempted to put an end to the disorder by claiming the episcopal property themselves. In time, however, believing the spoils of a deceased clergyman belonged to no individual, but to the church, the pope quite naturally claimed the goods of an archbishop, bishop, abbot, or any ecclesiastic who died.

Innocent IV took the first step in this direction in 1246 by declaring that the property of clergy dying intestate reverted to the Apostolic See. Little or nothing came of this decision until John XXII (1316-1334) laid claim to the spoils of a number of bishops.[8] By the fourteenth century the spoils formed one of the most noteworthy sources of revenue for the church.

Fruits During Vacancy. Inasmuch as the revenues of a benefice continued during a vacancy, the question arose as to who should be the recipient of these revenues. The magistrates claimed them on the grounds that a vacant benefice depended upon the protection of civil law, and, therefore, it was only just for the crown to claim some of the earnings.

Gregory the Great, however, declared all revenue of the vacant benefices to belong to the clergy in common. At first, the papacy claimed the right to the revenues during the vacancy, but only from those benefices that were filled by papal appointment. However, from the time of John XXII, the power of the papacy increased until nearly all appointments were made by the pope; and beginning with John XXII, the papacy took full advantage of the vacancies.

The pope's claim to the right of vacancies gave rise to a serious abuse: namely, extending the period of vacancy in order to gain more from the benefice.

It was Benedict XII who made it a point to prolong the vacancy so as to receive more income. This procedure led many to believe that the pope was more concerned about the income from the vacant benefice than providing a ministry for the faithful. Thus, to the extent that this was true, the pope defeated the purpose for which the papacy had been created.

However, this procedure was nothing more than placing the organization above the welfare of the people, and the popes were neither the first nor the last to do that!

Annates. The spoils, income during vacancy, and annates were like three links in a chain. The right of spoils was the right of the goods of the deceased; the fruits during vacancy were the right of the revenues during the vacancy; and the annates were the incomes from the benefices for the first year they had been filled. The annates were given biblical sanction by calling them "first fruits."

The right to collect annates was given, at first, by the popes to monks, bishops, or kings. Examples of this practice occur as early as the eleventh century; it became common in the following two centuries.[9] In A.D. 1216, the Archbishop of Canterbury obtained the annates of all the benefices of his province. Later, A.D. 1256, the King of England, Henry III, received (for a period of five years) all the annates of his kingdom.[10]

Clement V was the first to make use of annates to enrich the papacy. This, however, was only a temporary and local undertaking. It was John XXII, successor to Clement V, who extended the annates to the whole church.

A minor, yet significant, innovation in the scheme of annates developed in the fifteenth century when a considerable number of benefices were being united permanently with ecclesiastical corporations such as congregations, hospitals, or monasteries. This meant the benefices so united would never become vacant again. Thus, the pope no longer could claim revenue connected with vacancies. Therefore, the popes required the ecclesiastical bodies to which the benefices had been annexed, to pay at regular intervals—from eight to twenty years—the amount of services and annates previously due from such benefices at every vacancy.

This tax was known as *quindennia*. Such unions became so numerous that Pius II (1458-1464) felt compelled to issue a general decree calling upon the ecclesiastical bodies to which benefices had been joined to pay all petty fees, annates, or first fruits every fifteen years "in perpetuity."

With this type of arrangement the income for services and annates was assured, yet the usual papal expenses were eliminated!

The payment of annates was resisted from the outset. During the three years in which Clement V demanded annates from England, the citizens complained bitterly. A protest was raised in every country in which annates were demanded. On the eve of the Reformation in England, 1532, the Commons was petitioned to examine the annates or first fruits that were demanded of the British clergy.[11] The following year the restraint of these payments to Rome was made absolute by the direction of Henry VIII.[12]

Just as the right of vacancies encouraged longer vacancies, so the right of annates encouraged shorter tenure. The popes considered it wise to appoint older men to the well-to-do benefices, for the older a man was, the sooner the benefice would be vacant. This, in turn, meant another year's income for the pope.

In some cases men either too old or too ill to serve were appointed to the more lucrative benefices. In one case an ailing clergyman died within a few hours after he had arrived at his new appointment. Hence, the papacy was able to claim the spoils, the income during the vacancy, and the annates for two successive years.

This is another instance in which the spiritual needs of the people were neglected for the sake of financial gain to the papacy. Instead of existing to serve the churches and the people, it again appears that the papacy existed primarily for itself.

A second abuse encouraged by the system of annates was simony. In giving the first year's revenues, the incumbent actually paid his first year's income for his appointment to the benefice. If a man was unable to pay the price for his appointment, the Italian bankers were ready to make the necessary loan. As shall be seen, this simoniacal practice also encouraged the abuse known as "pluralities"—the holding of a number of benefices by one individual.

Expectations. The expectations were promises of ecclesiastical benefices, not vacant at the time, which would become vacant upon the death of the holders. It became customary under John XXII and Clement VI to appoint the number of "expectants" for a single office so that chances were sold down to the tenth degree.

The whole system was a species of ecclesiastical gambling in which each "expectant" took a risk on the life of the holder of a benefice and on the lives of other "expectants" ahead of himself. Naturally, the value of the tenth expectation was very small, while that of the first might be of great value, particularly if the holder of the benefice in question was a very old or sickly man.

Illegitimate Fruits. An income known as *fructus illicite percepte* was derived from clergymen who had gained illegitimately the revenue of benefices. For a number of reasons a man may have held a benefice uncanonically. It might have been because he was too young, or because he held without proper dispensation more than one benefice, or for a variety of other reasons. Legally the benefice was vacant and the man was not entitled to the revenues. When he sought dispensation for the future and absolution for the past, these fruits might be remitted to him in full. It was customary, however, to exact a portion of the wrongfully received income. By the time of John XXII this custom was almost universal. Often, the amount was the income of one year, but there was no established proportion.

One such case happened in 1238 when the nephew of the King of Scotland was holding certain benefices without apostolic dispensation. The pope ordered all the revenues that had been collected to be restored and converted to the aid of the Holy Land.[13] In 1283, however, Pope Martin IV granted a professor of theology dispensation for holding a benefice without full right and required only a tenth of the fruits to be given to the pope.[14] Still another bishop by the name of Robert was required to pay 600 marks sterling as satisfaction of fruits which he had received unlawfully from certain benefices for which he had lacked dispensation to serve.[15]

Services. The "services" or *servitia* were fees paid by bishops, abbots, and high prelates in general for nomination, consecration, and confirmation of office. The term "tax of *servitia*" dates from approximately 1250, but the practice was far older. As early as A.D. 595 Pope Gregory attempted to restrain the abuses he had witnessed and, in place of a fee, authorized voluntary offerings as tokens of gratitude.[16] In succeeding years the "token of gratitude" took on the characteristics of a required fee.

The tax of *servitia* made its appearance when cathedrals and abbeys were obliged to pay a fixed sum for each promotion of a bishop or abbot. Toward the end of the thirteenth century the *servitia* were divided into common *servitia,* small *servitia,* and secret *servitia.* The common *servitia* were for the pope and cardinals, usually amounting to one-third of the total; the small *servitia* were divided between the household of the pope and the households of the cardinals; and the secret *servitia* were the fees designed to purchase privately the favor of the pope or a cardinal.[17]

These fees were considered as offerings freely made. And, in a sense, there was freedom—one was free to pay the *servitia* or be excommunicated! In 1279, for example, the Archbishop of Canterbury, John Peckham, was obliged to pay 4000 marks to the Roman Curia. He was able to borrow this amount from bankers, but had to repay the loan within five months or be excommunicated. Later he remarked, "I would never have accepted episcopal consecration had I foreseen the terrible curse which was awaiting me." [18]

In 1326 the monk Richard was appointed abbot of St. Albans only to learn after the promotion that the *servitia* tax was 720 marks; and, at the rate of 5 florins per mark, it equaled 3600 florins. He was made to swear an oath upon the Gospels that he would pay this amount, and, in case of nonpayment, excommunication would follow.[19]

Once again, a form of simony made its appearance—exchanging money for nomination, consecration, and confirmation to a spiritual office. Undoubtedly, this encouraged corruption in the church. One's ability to pay the various fees overshadowed more important qualifications for the office. The system made wealth the criterion for promotion. Men of material wealth were able to gain control of great numbers of benefices and, in turn, could hire secular priests to minister to the people. Again, the faithful were exploited in the name of religion!

The Pallium. Originally, the pallium was a cloak of distinction and honor presented to a bishop or an archbishop. Its use goes back to A.D. 514, when Symmachus granted it to Theodore, Archbishop of Laureacus in Pannonia; and, possibly, as far back as A.D. 336 when something similar to the pallium was presented to Marcus, Bishop of Rome.[20]

In the eighth century, the pallium ceased to be an exceptional honor and became a badge of promotion awarded by the papacy. Pope Nicholas I made the pallium a necessity for every archbishop in A.D. 866 when he ordered that no archbishop could be enthroned or could consecrate the Eucharist until he had received the pallium from the Roman see.[21]

Complaints soon were raised, and the accusation was made charging the pallium had become a commercial transaction. Appeals were made to King Canute; he asked for reform in a letter to Rome A.D. 1027. He then assured his subjects that matters would be improved.[22]

But the reform did not last. At the beginning of the twelfth century, the English archbishop had to send money to Rome to obtain the pallium. John VIII even declared every archbishop deposed who did not get his pallium within three months.[23]

The income from the palliums was considerable. One device used to increase the income was to decrease the cost of the pallium. This was done by gradually reducing the size. Originally, it was a wool cloak, but it was later reduced to a ribbon, four inches wide, ornamented with a red cross.

The granting of the pallium, like annates and services, encouraged the practice of simony. Considering the high cost of the pallium and the fact that the bishops and archbishops were compelled to have the pallium before they were allowed to consecrate the Eucharist, be enthroned, or remain in office, it is clear that it was another subtle way of selling spiritual things for money.

Pluralities. A clergyman in possession of two or more benefices was considered to have a "plurality." Today, multiple-point fields—not generally desired by ministers—have become a necessity because of the shortage of leadership and overchurched communities. Previous to the Reformation, however, multiple-point fields were sought by the clergy for the revenue they produced.

At an early date it was forbidden for a man to serve in more than one place. Evidently, Ambrose thought it unlawful for a bishop to have two churches.[24] The Council of Chalcedon (A.D. 451) [25] and the Sixteenth Council of Toledo (A.D. 693) [26] frowned on more than one church per person. Provisions were renewed to render pluralities impossible, but the abuse continued to grow.

It was not uncommon for a single priest to hold as many as twelve benefices. John Mansel, court chaplain to Henry III, possessed as many as 700. In 1369, the Bishop of Ely was informed that certain clerks in his diocese held twenty benefices each.[27]

The purpose for which the papacy was created was defeated, again. Instead of protecting and serving the local parish and guiding the church from error, the popes, in their efforts to gain financial support, neglected the spiritual welfare of the people.

Papal Taxations

Before taxation could be successful, the subjects had to have money. Consequently, the papacy encouraged Italian bankers to lend the necessary money for taxes. Long tradition had made the taking of interest unethical and irreligious.

Nevertheless, the Italian bankers accompanied the papal agents with ready money when the loans were necessary. Priests, laymen, monks, and prelates often were compelled to borrow from the bankers to pay the various taxes imposed by the papacy. Even the king of England was, at times, heavily in their debt.

In the centuries just preceding the Reformation, there were five main taxes levied by the Pontifical State: (1) Peter's pence, (2) clergy tithes and income taxes, (3) apostolic tax, (4) procuration, and (5) visitation tax.

Peter's Pence. This tax, which originated as a gift, was collected from England, the Scandinavian kingdoms, Poland, and some other districts. It was known originally, as the denarius of

St. Peter, given first to the pope and to the English colony at Rome. In this form it was instituted by Ina, king of Wessex (A.D. 639-726), extended to Marcia by Offa II, king of that country (A.D. 784).[28] A letter of Pope Leo III (A.D. 797) indicates that Offa II promised to pay in perpetuity to St. Peter 365 *mancuses* annually.[29]

The Anglo-Saxon king, Ethelwulf, in A.D. 853, promised an annual gift of 300 mancuses, ". . . to be carried to Rome every year for the good of his soul." The gift was to be divided equally three ways: one part for buying oil to light St. Peter's Church on Easter Eve; one part to provide oil for St. Paul's Church; and one part for the universal apostolic pope.[30]

Any of the above-mentioned acts may have been the origin of Peter's pence. Beginning as a voluntary gift on the part of the kings, it soon was required of the people.

The laws of Edward and Guthrum (A.D. 921-938) required payment of Peter's pence or the payment of a fine. Edmund (A.D. 942-946) issued a law requiring church dues, Peter's pence, and plough alms, and, if one failed to comply, he was to be excommunicated. The laws of Edgar (A.D. 959-962) required a "hearth-penny" and, if it was not paid, the individual had to deliver it to Rome. The laws of Ethelred (A.D. 1008) required Peter's pence at a special Mass known as Peter's Mass. It was also made an enforced tax under King Canute, who, after visiting Rome, sent word back to England requiring—"The denarius of Peter should be paid on the feast of Peter. Whosoever shall not have paid it at that date must deliver it to the bishop, and in addition he must pay a fine." [31]

When fully collected, this tax affected every family within the kingdom. Nothing aroused the national feeling in England against Roman taxation more than did the Peter's pence. Oddly enough, however, even after Henry VIII had renounced the pope, the Peter's pence continued to be collected by the Crown until the time of Elizabeth I.

Voluntary gifts were replaced by an enforced tax. First, people were moved to contribute because of their concern for the English Christians living in Rome; then, various kings committed their people to the tax.

Clergy Tithes and Income Taxes. Clergy tithes, in their earliest form, were a tax levied on the revenue of ecclesiastical benefices by the kings to meet the expenses of the Crusades. The clergy soon objected to the tax, and after a number of councils had considered the issue, it was ordered, in 1215, that bishops were not to pay taxes to kings without having applied previously to Rome. The outcome, of course, was that popes, rather than kings, became recipients of the tithes.

Tithes from the clergy not only helped to finance the Crusades, but also helped to pay for other "holy" wars. These tithes were a tenth of the gross,[32] increased by the Council of Lyons (1245) to half of the revenue, for a three-year period.[33] Boniface VIII formulated the papal authority in this matter of ecclesiastical property by declaring the Apostolic See to have absolute power over the property, enabling it to exact any part of it.[34]

Because of the tax-tithe the clergy were almost helpless, forcing many to pawn altar furniture, to borrow money at high interest, and to pledge their growing crops. If they failed, they were threatened with punishment by the king and excommunication by the pope.

Income taxes imposed by the papacy were similar to the clergy tithes. They also began in connection with the Crusades. Lay rulers had set a precedent, in 1166 and in 1188, when the kings of England and France levied a tax from their lay and clerical subjects for the purpose of a crusade. Innocent III was the first pope to levy the income tax on his clerical subjects when, in 1199, he commanded them to pay one-fortieth of their ecclesiastical incomes for one year in aid of the Holy Land.[35]

In reading these appeals for help, one is impressed with the way they call for voluntary contributions based on a suggested percentage. However, word for the payment of the tax seldom reached the clergy in the form of a request; it came as a demand!

Neither the clergy nor the laity were very willing to respond to the appeals from Rome unless they were compelled to do so. One fact cannot be escaped: namely, the church of the Middle Ages was controlled by an organization which many of the faithful were unwilling to support. If the papacy had not had the means whereby it could compel the people to give, it would have ceased to exist—or, it would have had to reorganize radically.

Apostolic Tax. From an early period monasteries and kingdoms had been "recommended" to Peter or Paul, that is, placed under their guardianship. But until the close of the eighth century, it had not occurred to anyone that the apostles should be paid for their watchful care. When the monastery of Lacques was founded in A.D. 780, however, a provision was made for a payment to the Church of St. Peter in recognition of the protection exercised by the apostle.[36] After this, many charters for both monasteries and villages contained a financial provision for the guardian apostle.

In the twelfth century, when monasteries no longer feared pillage, the apostolic tax underwent a new interpretation, being employed for exemption from episcopal control.

Urban II was the first to allow the power of purchasing "liberty" or independence of the jurisdiction of the bishops. Thereupon, a considerable number of monasteries, which were not yet free, immediately offered to buy their independence. As could be expected, the bishops did not approve, but the protests of the bishops availed nothing.

Kingdoms also became census payers of the Apostolic See. Princes, wishing to be independent of St. Peter who had been their protector, agreed to make a cash settlement. After a number of princes and monasteries had volunteered to settle their accounts with the apostle, the papacy set out to induce others to settle, too.

England, again, became a field for taxation by Rome. Innocent III was able to force John Lackland to subject England to this taxation. Lackland agreed to pay an annual tribute of 1000 marks to the Apostolic See, contracting for all his successors to do the same.[37]

Procurations. In the Middle Ages, while they were traveling, lords had the right to demand a certain amount of entertainment from their subjects. Ecclesiastical officials adopted the custom, calling it the "right of procuration." Bishops or archbishops had the right to be lodged by the parish priest when they visited for the purpose of supervision. This proved to be a heavy expense to the priest, since the bishops and archbishops usually were accompanied by a sizable delegation.

The papacy realized an income from this tax in two ways. First, in the twelfth and thirteenth centuries the popes received procurations from certain places and priests when they traveled. The rate varied with the rank of the envoy and the income of the priests who were visited.

Second, the papacy realized an income from procurations by granting dispensations allowing the official to neglect the visitation. Previously, it had been the rule that procurations could be collected only after visitation. But Boniface VIII, and later Clement V, authorized the archbishop of Bourges to collect procurations by deputy. When the archbishop died in 1316, several dioceses in his province had not been visited. John XXII appointed commissioners to collect from them for the apostolic treasury.

In other instances, prelates who were allowed to collect their procurations by deputies made voluntary gifts of large sums to the pope. Under Clement VI, this latter innovation became common. The prelates usually gave to the treasury "freely and spontaneously" one-half of the procurations secured through deputies.[38]

Visitation Tax. This tax fell exclusively on the higher clergy who were to visit periodically the tombs of the apostles. As early as the eighth century this duty was laid upon bishops in and near Rome.[39]

From the eleventh century, before archbishops could receive the pallium, they had to promise to make regular visits to Rome. The frequency of the visits varied in proportion to the length of the journey. Italian prelates came every year; English, once every three years.

Compared to the cost of the journey, the tax itself was not large. However, there were severe laws which governed payments. If a payment was not made on time, a collector levied the tax. A delinquent payer could be excommunicated and otherwise penalized.[40]

Church Courts

On the eve of the Reformation the transactions in church courts had become a scandal. In the Petition of the Commons, an appeal was made for relief from abuses in church courts. The people were exploited in the church courts through (1) excessive fees, (2) unjust fines, (3) probation of wills, and (4) appeals to Rome. Either directly or indirectly these exploits meant money for the papacy.

Excessive Fees. The courts were under the control of the clergy, and it was easy for one to commit a slight error and find himself on trial. In fact, many were taken to court who never were found guilty! Nevertheless, the court fees had to be paid, and—as both the Petition of the Commons [41] and "The Supplication of Beggars" [42] point out—the fees were excessive.

It is apparent the clergy had lost sight of the purpose of the courts. Laws were used, not to bring justice, but to yield fees to the church. The church courts, which were established to insure justice for all, now provided the means by which injustice was made not only possible but honorable.

Unjust Fines. The Petition to the Commons and "The Supplication of the Beggars" call attention to unreasonable fines imposed on the people by the clergy, who brought them into court.

Petition Number XII reveals the case of a layman accused of heresy who might as well have considered himself guilty before the trial began, for the learned clergy could confound the average layman in spiritual matters.[43]

Thus, whether a man was guilty or not, the court fees and fines were charged against him. The clergy sacrificed truth and justice and service for financial gain.

Probation of Wills. Soon after Constantine decreed that property might be bequeathed to the church, the privilege was misused. At times, the clergy appeared more interested in the death of an individual than in his personal welfare.

The sixth petition of the Commons dealt with unreasonable delays and high fees in probating wills. The courts were accused of having an unnecessary number of judges, scribes, apparitors, summoners, appraisers, and other ministers who, ". . . coveting so much their own private lucres," [44] showed little concern for the public.

Quite early, the people sought the help of the clergy in making out their wills. The clergy frequently yielded to the temptation of exploiting the faithful in these transactions. But when the clergy gained control of the church courts, the exploitation ran rampant.

Appeals to Rome. Since final authority resided in the papal court, people often were compelled to go to Rome for licenses, dispensations, and the settlements of various matters.

The basic costs were unreasonable, and after many unnecessary delays, a man usually yielded to the temptation of paying extra to speed up the transaction.[45]

The elaborate organization within the papal court accounted for much of the excessive cost; and the elaborate organization was due primarily to a questionable system of raising money—the selling of offices. Boniface IX (1389-1404) inaugurated the practice of selling offices to raise money. It did not become a rich source of income until fifty years later in the pontificate of Calixtus III (1455-1458).

Pius II (1458-1464) began to increase the number of curial employees and to organize them into new colleges. Each college received, in common, certain fees and revenues which were divided among the members. The increase of fees and other dues in the second half of the fifteenth century was due mainly to the necessity of supporting the numerous additions to the curial bureaucracy.[46]

When Sixtus IV (1471-1484) wished to raise extra money, he increased his secretaries from 6 to 24 and required each to pay 2,600 florins for the office. In 1486, the creation of 71 collectors of the seal produced 20,000 florins [48]; Alexander VI (1503) raised funds by creating 80 new offices and selling them for 760 ducats apiece; and Julius II formed a "college" of 101 scribes who paid a total of 74,000 ducats for their offices.[49]

Under Leo X (1513-1521) the sale of offices provided nearly one-sixth of the ordinary income of the papal budget.[50] He appointed 60 chamberlains from whom he received 90,000 ducats and also appointed 140 squires who returned to him 112,000 ducats.[51]

A record appearing in the Vatican Archives, dated July 20, 1514, shows a variety of offices—a total of 784—that were sold, indicating the inevitable high overhead of the papal court.[52]

These offices became the personal property of the owners and could be sold to successors. In such transactions, the pope levied a commission of five per cent.

The creation of these offices placed a tremendous burden on the people who were compelled to go to the papal court. Those who paid the pope for the particular office counted on gaining back much more as they waited on the public, and, in addition, the public was expected to pay all fees connected with each transaction.

Every document requesting an absolution or dispensation, plus every will and probate, had to pass through an incredible number of hands. Each time the document was handled, a fee was imposed. Cases are on record where briefs had cost from twenty-four to forty-one times the amount of the legitimate official charges.[53]

Throughout the history of the church the presence of the clergy has been made necessary during life's crises. However, the general tendency has been for the clergy to exact a fee or "gift" for services rendered during these times of crisis.

Undoubtedly, the church courts were created to render a necessary service in time of crisis, but the greed of the clergy led them to use the courts for their own ends, rather than make themselves expendable for the faithful.

The financial transactions of the church relating to vacancies, taxations, and church courts were very practical methods of raising funds. They had only indirect bearing on the doctrines of the church; consequently, motives played little part in the individual's response. The response was made out of compulsion to obey certain laws.

These methods of fund raising—probably more correctly called schemes—were important elements that helped to foment the Reformation in England.

IV

The Middle Ages
(Motives)

During the Middle Ages, a series of doctrinal developments led to questionable motivations in giving money to the church, which, in turn, stirred Martin Luther to protest against the distortions of these doctrines.

So, financial matters between Rome and England played a part in the reform of the church in England; but, on the continent, motives in fund raising helped to stimulate the Reformation. Specifically, it was the motivation and the theological implications in the sale of indulgences and the adoration of relics which helped to arouse the reformers.

To appreciate the sacramental value involved in the purchase of indulgences, in the adoration of relics, and in the pilgrimages to holy places, one must understand the related theological beliefs that had developed.

Medieval theology is a theology of merit. The way to God and eternal blessedness, as stated by the most prominent theologian of the Middle Ages, Thomas Aquinas, is that of merit. Aquinas indicates, "Man attains it [blessedness] by many movements [acts] which are called merits." [1] However, this does not exclude grace. In fact, Aquinas stresses, salvation is from God. For him, and for the medieval church, there was no contradiction between the idea of grace and the idea of merit. Any merit which a man gains he gains because of the grace of God. Yet, to attain blessedness a man must gain merit. Herein lies the sacramental value of good works in the theology of Thomas Aquinas.

Revenue-Producing Doctrines

Very early in the Christian church the sacramental value of good works was strengthened because of the influence of the Old Testament conception of "righteousness." In the first half of the second century there were no great personalities to take the place of the Apostle Paul. New Testament literature was not available, generally, and Christian teachers and writers had to depend upon pre-New Testament literature for inspiration and direction. The Epistle of Clement reveals the prevalence of the Old Testament teachings in this early period. In Clement's Epistle, one hundred and twenty references are from the Old Testament; only a dozen passages show a knowledge of the New Testament.[2]

In this early century, the Old Testament conception of righteousness cast a shadow over the "righteousness of faith" which the New Testament sets forth.

Augustine and Chrysostom are considered, generally, to have been evangelical theologians; however, some of their sermons—as we noted in Chapter II—contain the idea of legalism and good works.

"The Works of Monks," by Augustine, encourages the faithful to give with heaven's reward in mind.[3] At another point he claims that alms and fasting supply the two wings for prayers.[4]

Chrysostom makes an even stronger case for the merits of almsgiving, saying, "If then thou also desirest to escape the flame, lay up alms beforehand, and so thou wilt not even taste of that fire." [5]

Obviously, the doctrine of the medieval church—salvation through merit—had a definite place in the church from as early as the second and third centuries.

Another doctrinal development that opened the way for selling indulgences was that of purgatory, indulgences being for the remission from purgatorial punishment, which takes place in the intermediate state after death where the souls of the saved are purified.

The growth and development of the penance formula must be understood before one can comprehend what finally took place in the selling of indulgences.

In the ancient church—as early as Tertullian and Cyprian—a serious lapse into sin involved separation from the Christian fellowship. Some, under the pressure of persecution, denied the faith. Readmission was granted by public confession made in the presence of the whole congregation and by a demonstration of true repentance in performing certain satisfactions, such as fasting and almsgiving. The congregation decided on the amount of satisfaction necessary and, also, determined whether the individual was to be readmitted. If, for some sound reason, the prescribed satisfaction could not be carried out, another satisfaction might be substituted. This allowance for substitution was one of the origins of the system of indulgences.

In the course of time, the confession of sins was made in private to a priest rather than to the whole congregation, and the imposed satisfaction placed in the hands of the priest.

In an attempt to hold priests to some standard, lists of sins with the corresponding appropriate satisfactions were published. About the seventh century there arose the practice of commuting satisfactions, that is, one satisfaction or penance was substituted for another.

This, then, was the actual beginning of the doctrine of indulgences—a relaxation of ecclesiastical penalties which had been imposed according to the regular custom in cases of discipline.[6]

A theological development, without which the church might

have been unable to abuse the doctrine of indulgences, was the idea of the treasury (or storehouse) of merits. The merits of the saints—especially of the martyrs—and, above all, the merits of Christ had formed a storehouse of merits from which the church might draw.

The idea had developed over many centuries, but Thomas Aquinas established it in a system of theology. First, he defended the proposition that one man could fulfill satisfactory punishment for another.[7] Then, he said, the merits of those who had suffered without reason—especially the merits of Christ —were such as to exceed the entire debt of punishment due to those living at any moment. Clement VI gave official approval to the theory in a bull, dated January 27, 1343, in which he said:

> The whole human kind might have been saved by one single drop of the blood of Christ, but having shed so much, and certainly not for nothing, this excess formed an inexhaustible church treasure, which was still increased by the not superfluous merits of the saints and martyrs. The pope is the keeper of this treasure, and may dispense of it to any degree without fear of exhausting it.[8]

The concept of purgatory opened the way for a new application of the idea of indulgences. Indulgences as relaxations of imposed penances of satisfactions were overshadowed by the more valuable indulgence which, thanks to the storehouse of merits, in the sight of God was the equivalent of the temporal punishments due.[9]

The real value of indulgences was their assurance of remission of penalties due after absolution, penalties that may or may not have been imposed by a priest. It was this innovation that opened the way for the greatest abuse. Significantly, Luther's theses were primarily an attack against the idea of indulgences being available for the penalties imposed by God, rather than by a priest.

Trade in Indulgences. Papal indulgences were of profit to others before they became a significant factor in the support of the papacy. They emerged along two lines. First, there were limited indulgences granted to seekers of pardon for visiting a certain church. Individual churches were aided by these pilgrimages because of the voluntary offerings presented by the faithful. If the papacy profited at all, it was only through the regular taxation of bulls which allowed the indulgences. Second, indulgences developed in connection with the Crusades. Here real commercialization began! Also, these indulgences were not limited to a few days or years, but were plenary—that is, the remission of the entire temporal punishment due to sin.

As early as A.D. 1095, Pope Urban II promised full indulgences to all who engaged in the First Crusade. In the following century indulgences were conferred upon those who contributed toward the cost of a crusade. Eugene III (in 1145 or 1146) offered an indulgence of one-seventh of required penance to those who contributed sufficient alms to a specific cause.

A unique system evolved in 1166 when indulgences were granted for paying a tax imposed by Henry II in response to a papal appeal for aid in behalf of the Holy Land. Those who paid this tax would be relieved by one-third of the enjoined penance. This practice set a precedent, and in the years to come the promise of partial indulgences for contributions placed in chests by those truly penitent became a common papal expedient.[10]

The summons of Pope Innocent III to a crusade in 1215 allowed remission even in the case of one who could not go himself, but who financed the trip for another.[11]

Boniface VIII took advantage of the outburst of popular enthusiasm and religious zeal to establish a year of Jubilee in 1300.

The crusading age was past, but the spirit which animated the Crusades still survived in Europe. Boniface promised indulgences to those who made the pilgrimage to Rome and who deposited a certain sum on the altar.[12]

According to one writer, not fewer than 200,000 strangers passed the year of 1300 in Rome. A "moderate estimation" indicates about 15,000,000 golden gilders were paid that year.[13]

The rich harvest from the first year of Jubilee, undoubtedly, led Clement VI to believe a year of Jubilee should be held every fifty years. In his Jubilee bull, he ordered the angels of paradise to release from purgatory the souls of those who might die on their way to Rome.[14]

Boniface IX (1389-1402) needed money, desperately, and went to extreme lengths to gain it. He, too, instituted a year of Jubilee and offered indulgences to those who would pay one-third of the traveling expenses in lieu of making the pilgrimage.

Pope Sixtus IV (1471-1484), by a bull of 1476, made into an article of faith the widespread belief that indulgences are available for souls in purgatory.[15]

But it was the bull of Julius II, dated January, 1510, which sparked Luther's revolt seven years later. In this commission the pope made no mention of repentance and confession as a condition for gaining an indulgence, but only of payment. And, for an extra sum, the sinner could choose his own confessor!

The system finally offended Martin Luther, during the reign of Leo X, when Leo needed money and opened his spiritual treasury of merits—the superfluous merits of the saints and the merit of Christ's death—and offered them to be applied toward the sinner's debts. Commissioners were appointed for a general distribution—what appeared to many to be a sale—of indulgences throughout Roman Catholic Europe.

A young man by the name of Albert had gone into debt heavily in purchasing the position of Archbishop of Mainz.

From the banking house of Fugger at Augsburg, Albert had borrowed a sizable amount.[16] Leo granted Albert the contract as commissioner of Germany with the understanding that half of the money collected in the sale of indulgences was to go to the banking house of Fugger to pay the note; the other half was to be remitted to Rome. The bargain was concluded in 1515 and began to be executed in 1517.

John Tetzel, a Dominican monk, was appointed to collect in Saxony. In the course of his sermons while selling indulgences, he is reported to have said:

> Indulgences are the most precious and the most
> noble of God's gifts. Come, and I will give you
> letters, all properly sealed, by which even the sins
> that you intend to commit may be pardoned.
> I would not change my privileges for those of St.
> Peter in Heaven; for I have saved more souls by
> my indulgences than the apostle by his sermons.[17]

Tetzel also assured his listeners indulgences would avail not only for the living, but for the dead. For that, repentance was not even necessary. Then, he would place the destiny of those in purgatory in the hands of his hearers:

> Priest! noble! merchant! wife! youth! maiden! Do
> you not hear your parents and your other friends
> who are dead, and who cry from the bottom of the
> abyss: We are suffering horrible torments! A trifling
> alms would deliver us; you can give it, and you will
> not! [18]

Martin Luther attempted to stop this practice by writing privately to several bishops to entreat their interferences, but none would move. Luther was determined to force the question before public opinion and, on October 31, 1517, affixed ninety-five theses to the door of Wittenberg Church, calling into question the current papal interpretations of indulgences and the right to sell them. The Reformation in Germany and on the rest of the continent followed.

Relics. From the second century, relics of martyrs were held in high regard. In the third century, miracles began to be associated with them, and since then the veneration of relics has been encouraged by the Roman Catholic Church. In the sixteenth century, the Council of Trent defined the doctrine concerning relics:

> If the clothes, the kerchiefs, and even the very
> shadows of the saints, whilst yet on earth, banished
> disease and restored health and vigour, who will
> have the hardihood to deny that God can still work
> the same wonders by the holy ashes, the bones and
> other relics of his saints who are in glory? [19]

Between the time the early Christians gathered up the bones of Polycarp (in the second century) and the pronouncement of the Council of Trent, the church received a sizable income by displaying various relics.

In the fourth century, Gregory of Nyssa, speaking of the remains of the martyr St. Theodore, said a spiritual blessing would result in carrying off some of the dust from the resting place of the saint.[20]

Later, forgiveness from sins and deliverance from purgatory could be attained by making a pilgrimage to adore the relics. The *Mirabilia Romae,* a guidebook for pious travelers, went through nineteen Latin and twelve German editions before the year 1500. It promised forgiveness of all sins, both guilt and penalty, to all who went to the Lateran Church and worshiped there. The pilgrim who went to the High Altar of St. Peter's Church with good intentions was freed from all sins.[21]

For such benefits as these, it was only natural for the faithful to show their appreciation with gifts of money. The practice of venerating relics and paying money for the privilege grew until it became an important method by which the church was supported.

Financial transactions relating to relics may be classified into three general groups: (1) the selling and buying of relics, (2) the papal fee for declaring the authenticity of the relic, and (3) the oblations presented when the faithful looked upon or touched the relic.

Peddling relics was a business of no small concern. Dealers in old bones often sold the remains of animals as the human bones of some saint. Augustine, denouncing certain impostors wandering about in the habit of monks, describes them as making profit by the sale of spurious relics.[22]

Those who returned from the Crusades with relics had cargo of greater value than those who returned with mere jewels and gold.

As one might expect, the papacy found a way to profit by the relics: namely, by exacting a fee from the possessor of a relic in return for a bull which declared its authenticity. The fact that parties claimed to possess identical relics created no problem; apparently, the papacy was willing to declare almost any article authentic if the fee was a substantial amount.[23]

The gifts of the faithful in the presence of a relic were, of course, the main financial consideration. Relics attracted worshipers to the holy places and the presentation of money and gifts in kind was an essential part of the veneration.

Miracles of every description are reported, and nothing increased the monetary value of a relic so much as accompanying miracles. An example of the way in which a new or miracle-producing relic increased the income of the church or monastery is found in the records from Canterbury. In 1213 the Convent was returned from France to England, and in 1220 the relics of the saint were transferred to a new shrine in the chapel, built for its reception. In one year, 1220, the offerings increased fivefold.[24]

Over the years the relics have accumulated until the duplication is difficult to explain. Some saints have had several skeletons. That of St. Denis, for example, once existed in duplicate, having a third head in Prague and a fourth head in Hamburg; and Munich could boast of one of his hands.[25]

The following list of relics have received the infallible approval of various popes:

> Splinters and nails from the cross.
> The sponge which was lifted to Christ's mouth.
> The purple coat which was thrown over Christ's shoulders by the mocking soldiers.
> The crown of thorns.
> Thorns from the crown.
> The cup from which Christ drank when he instituted the Lord's Supper.
> Specimens of the hair of the Virgin Mary—some blond, some red, some brown, and some black.
> Remaining bread from the Last Supper.
> The dice used by the soldiers in casting lots.
> The unseamed tunic.
> Shirts of the Virgin, her wedding ring, slippers, swaddling clothes.
> The carpenter tools of Joseph.
> One of the thirty pieces of silver.
> The empty purse of Judas.
> The perch on which the cock crew three times.
> Pilate's basin.
> The bones of the ass on which the entry into Jerusalem was made.
> Moses' staff, the one used to part the Red Sea.
> Manna from the desert.
> Noah's beard.
> A piece of rock from which Moses drew water.

The Council of Trent attempted to remove fees and charges connected with relics and decreed no new relics would be recognized "unless the bishop of the diocese has taken cognizance and approved them." [26]

Absolutions and Dispensations. Income was realized by granting absolutions and dispensations in special cases.

Innocent III (1196-1216) issued the first bull granting absolution by paying a sum of money. To those who had made a vow to go on a crusade and found that they were unable to do so, he granted absolution from their vow upon the payment of a certain amount of money.[27]

Gradually, the sale of absolution gave rise to a new industry known as the "letter of confession." The letter of confession was a diploma which conferred on the holder the right to choose a confessor who, in turn, would grant absolution.

Dispensations were given as exemptions from an ecclesiastical law or from any impediments created by the law. They were associated closely with absolutions. To wit: dispensations were given, often, to those who had been excommunicated. For a price the pope would allow absolution to be given without making the trip to Rome.

An example of such a dispensation is given by André Lagarde.[28] A husband, whose wife had been seduced by a priest, had cut off the priest's nose. Thereupon, the husband became subject to excommunication. Innocent III, however, authorized the man to obtain absolution from his bishop, but he also obliged him to give, for this dispensation, the money which the journey to Rome would have cost him.

Dispensations relating to marriages were very common. A dispensation was required in the case of marriages between blood relatives. Such dispensations were quite frequent; for, according to the regulations made by the popes, relatives up to the seventh degree were prohibited from marrying. A case in point was Viscount Cardona and his wife who discovered in 1237—after many years of married life—that they were related within the forbidden degrees. They petitioned the pope, who granted a dispensation providing the viscount would agree to furnish forty knights for a year's service against the Moors in Spain.[29]

In a summarizing examination of those methods of support which were motivated by certain doctrines of the church, significant facts present themselves and familiar patterns recur. First, the doctrine of salvation by merit encouraged abuse. Medieval theology broke down at its weakest point, and its weakest point grew out of an attempt to make works central in the whole plan of salvation. Merit grew to be an indispensable factor in salvation, becoming one of the pillars on which medieval theology was constructed. The doctrine of works of supererogation—and with it the alleged storehouse of merits—gave the church an available stock of goodness to be used for appropriation to the penitent. The next, and natural, step was for the church to demand a price for the commodity which she had at her disposal. The final abuse was not a far step from all that had preceded. The pope, being the vice-gerent of God—and, therefore, the one with proper authority to exercise the powers of God—took the final step and claimed to remit what God had imposed.

The first fact which comes out of a study of the financial support of the church of the Middle Ages is this: Abuses were made possible through a previous distortion of the gospel.

A second fact, which has occurred often enough to become a pattern, is this: As money-making becomes more necessary the spiritual leaders lose sight of the primary purpose of the church and their ministries. They, as a part of an institution—created for the glory of God and service to man—have exploited the religious convictions of man in order to support the institution. Hence, the institution, rather than a means to a higher end, became an end in itself.

The third fact: The medieval period gives further evidence that the voluntary principle of support is directly dependent upon the faith of the people. When they believed in the program seeking their support, their voluntary offerings were forthcoming. The evidence at hand further indicates this fact: either the papacy had no faith in the voluntary method of support or the people showed their lack of faith in the papacy by failing to support it voluntarily.

A fourth fact: Simony was practiced in a number of ways— by selling offices, benefices, rank, position, absolution, and dispensations. The chances of an individual to secure either position or salvation depended, not on qualifications, consecration, or faith, but rather on his ability to produce the necessary money.

Finally, the various financial transactions of the church of the Middle Ages gives further evidence that the financial need of the church is one of her most vulnerable points. Again and again, money dealings by, and within, the church have been a bitter offense to the faithful. This one area of church life cried for reform throughout the medieval period, and—it might be added—cries for reform today.

V

The Reformation and
Later in Europe

Three significant facts relative to church finance emerged from a study of the Reformation. First, the Reformation itself was —in part—a culmination of protests against abuses in financial matters of the church. Second, the motives underlying the protests in the two reform movements—in England and on the Continent—differed radically. Third, although financial abuses helped greatly to foment the Reformation, the movement itself did little to produce an immediate program for supporting the church which was in harmony with the voluntary principle of the New Testament.

In preceding chapters an attempt was made to substantiate the first statement. The multiple ways by which Rome had been taking money from England under the guise of religion did more than anything else to induce King Henry VIII to break with the pope. Likewise, on the Continent it was the unmitigated trade in indulgences and relics, as well as the immorality which wealth had encouraged among the clergy, that first incited the reformers.

The second statement, claiming that the motives behind the two reform movements differed radically, hardly needs verification. In a word, the Reformation in England was basically political and economic; on the Continent, especially in Germany, it was religious. England's break with Rome was motivated politically and economically; reform in doctrine came later. On the Continent, however, the motivation for the reform movement was basically religious. Although Luther did not, at first, object to the granting of indulgences, he was offended by the pope's *selling* of indulgences reputed to cover penalties imposed by God. As he continued to re-examine the New Testament, especially the writings of Paul, Luther was led to see that the abuse in indulgences was not only wrong, but that the doctrine of the church which motivated them was not in keeping with the gospel of the New Testament.

Out of this "rediscovery" of the gospel, one would expect the reformers to set forth methods of church support in keeping with the principles of the New Testament. But such was not the case! The principles were stated; but, generally, the implications of those principles in the area of church support were overlooked.

The reform in England, at first, did little to remove abuses in church finance. The financial exploits associated with the monasteries were, of course, curtailed because the monasteries were dissolved. But the infamous system of taxation and tithing continued; and, for a time, indulgences, under some variation, continued to be purchased.

The reform movement on the Continent checked some of the financial exploitations. At best, however, church support was reformed only partially. The sale of indulgences was removed and the adoration of relics was curtailed because a doctrine of justification by faith had swept aside a doctrine of alms, works, prayers, and pilgrimages. Yet, when one looks to the reformers for a constructive and consistent program for financing the church, he is disappointed. Both in England and on the Continent, the voluntary principle, which is so basic in the Christian faith, was usually lacking in the finances of the Protestant Church.

A picture of church finance in England, Scotland, Ireland, and Germany in the century or century-and-a-half following the Reformation can be drawn using these categories: (1) the tithe system, (2) church rates, and (3) state support.

The Tithe System

One of the most deeply ingrained methods of supporting the church, especially the Church of England, at the time of the Reformation was an elaborate and compulsory system of tithing. The historical development of this system to the Reformation has been outlined in a former chapter.[1] The purpose of this chapter is to indicate: (1) the intricate details of the system as it was carried out in the Church of England, (2) the system on the Continent, and (3) the attitude of the people toward the system.

Intricate Details of the Tithing System. In 1677 Simon Degge wrote a book, entitled, *The Parsons Counsellor,*[2] which was a guide to ministers in the Church of England regarding all matters with which they might be confronted. The last half of the book deals, specifically, with the laws of tithes and tithing.

Some canonists divided tithes into two kinds, predial and personal. The predial tithes were subdivided as mediate and immediate. Predial immediate tithes were those tithes of "Corn Hay Wood Herbs and all other things, that either come from the ground by manurance, or of its own Nature." [3] Tithes predial mediate were the tithes "of all manner of Cattel and other things that receive their nourishment from the ground." [4] However, Mr. Degge uses the division of the Canon Lawyers, which were "predial"—those that grow from the ground; "mixt" (mixed)—those that arise from livestock; and "personal"—those that are produced through the labor of man.[5] Tithes were divided further into great tithes and small tithes. "And in this division Corn Hay and Wood are all accounted gross or great

Tithes." [6] Small tithes were "all manner of Tithes of Gardens Herbs Roots Fruits Flax Hemp Hops Rape, and all other Predial Personal and Mixt Tithes." [7]

The manner and form of payment, for the most part, was governed by the "Custom of the place." [8] Custom carried much authority. The term "time out of mind" often is used to denote custom. Also, custom was to be observed if it had been "constant without interruption, and perpetual from the time whereof the memory of Man is not to the contrary. . . ." [9] Various statutes created by Parliament under Henry VIII and Elizabeth upheld the authority of custom and prescription in the manner of tithing.[10] Custom bowed to Common Law,[11] and Common Law bowed to the "Law of God." [12]

As a general rule, a farmer was not required to pay a tithe on food consumed by himself or his family.

> If a Man gather green pease to spend in his
> House, and there spend them in his Family,
> no Tithes shall be paid for the same; but if he
> gather them to sell or to feed Hogs, there Tithes
> shall be paid for them.[13]

> Of young Pigeons in Dovecoats or in Pigeonholes
> about a man's house, Tithe shall be paid, if they
> be sold; but if they be spent in the Family,
> no Tithe shall be paid for them.[14]

Likewise, building materials taken from a man's land, if used on his property, were not tithable. If they were sold, however, they were to be tithed.[15]

Prescribing the system further, materials taken from the farm that ultimately would go to help provide tithable produce were not tithed. Feed for the beasts that pulled the plow, likewise, was not on the list since the beasts produced the harvest which was to be tithed. Trees were tithed according to their age and use. Trees of over twenty years' growth, when cut and sold, were to be tithed.

If a farmer wanted to avoid detailed bookkeeping, he would do as little buying and selling as possible, since intricate formulas were used to arrive at values. For example, the tithe on a cow—bought or sold—was determined by the growth and potential productive power of the animal at the time of sale.

The farmer was encouraged to plow new land by a statute which declared the land and produce tithe-free for a period of seven years. By the same law, the parson was protected in that a farmer could not turn back the land to waste: ". . . the Parson, Vicar, &c. shall not lose his Tithe by the ill husbandry of the Parishioner." [16]

Obviously, it was difficult to tithe the animals when they numbered either less than ten or a figure not divisible by ten. Therefore, both the canonists and the judges of Common Law agreed on a formula which allowed the parson various cash amounts on a specified number of animals.[17]

When a farmer moved his livestock from one parish to another to graze, he ran into tithe troubles; for the tithe had to be divided between the two parish churches, according to the time the sheep or cattle were kept in the two areas.[18] The man who caught a fish within the bounds of another parish had a greater problem than merely cleaning the fish, for the law read:

> . . . if the Parishioner of one parish had his fish in
> another, the Tithes are divided between the
> Parson of the Parish where the fisher lives, and
> the other where he landed his fish; but if the
> Parishioner land his fish in the Parish where he
> himself dwells, then the Rector of that Parish has
> the whole Tithes.[19]

The law also protected the farmer from the clergy. If the parson or vicar were to enter a man's property and sort out the tithe, he would be considered a trespasser. In addition, the farmer's crops and pasture were protected by law from the hungry beasts which the parson brought with him with which to haul away the tithe.

Mr. Degge's book deals, primarily, with the tithes of farmers. However, tithes were required by law of those who were on wages and salary. These tithes were designated as "personal" tithes. The tithes from hunting, hawking, fishing, and fowling were considered personal tithes, "these things being obtained by the labour and industry of the Party." [20] One was to pay a personal tithe or a tenth part of all his clear gains after deducting all charges and expenses. If a man made no gain on his merchandise, obviously, no tithe was to be paid.

The apparent need of requiring a tithe on merchandising, wages, and salaries presented itself soon after popery was abolished in England, causing a drastic drop in the support of the clergy in London. Consequently, during the time of King Henry VIII, the clergy made application to the Parliament and obtained an Act which provided for lawful tithing of all income received from houses, shops, warehouses, cellars, and stables within the city. These tithes were demanded and expected of all except usurers and prostitutes, but even their personal tithes were accepted, readily, if they professed themselves penitent.[21]

Seventeenth-century England brought to its culmination a tithing system that left no one untouched. This involved system was based on civil laws, ecclesiastical canons, and custom. Ironically, all the laws, canons, and customs had developed from false premises. Misinterpretation of each former decision only added to the falsehood. Once scholarship started examining the sources, especially the writings of the early Fathers, the system was doomed.

Tithing on the Continent. The development of tithing on the Continent was similar to that in England. Tithing continued in

Germany and the other countries after the Reformation, but the basic conceptions of the reform movement, naturally, threatened tithing as an enforced system. Luther's doctrine of the priesthood of believers tended to give the common man greater independence. Then, too, Luther had expressed, publicly, his approval of many of the proposals in the Twelve Articles of the peasants, in which three significant propositions were presented under the second article. First, the peasants set forth their beliefs that tithing was established by the Old Testament and fulfilled in the New Testament. Second, they held that a tithe, which they called the "just" tithe, was to be given of the grain only. Third, the "just" tithe was to help the poor as well as to support the pastor.[22] The importance of this article lies in its attempt to make tithing conform to biblical teachings.

Luther supported the secular authorities in the Peasants' War; yet, he apparently approved of the second article, for it somewhat represents the pattern that was followed in many Lutheran churches. The functions of the ecclesiastical government included the care of the poor, support of the ministry, and the maintenance of schools in the Protestant German States.

Zwingli, also, made a strong attack on the ecclesiastical system of tithing. He declared the tithes to be merely voluntary offerings. The basis of his statement was that nothing was binding on the conscience of Christians which was not commanded in Scripture.[23]

Tithing continued on the Continent, but it was not enforced as rigidly as in England. Revenues from ecclesiastical property, under the direction of the secular rulers, provided most of the support.

Attitudes of the Laity Toward the System. Soon after the Reformation, a growing number of people revolted against compulsory tithing. Some protested on religious grounds, others on practical grounds. The Anabaptists, and later the Quakers, earnestly desired a return to a church that was more in conformity with the New Testament. They opposed tithing, claiming it violated Christian principles. Others, who had bought or inherited land with a tithe lien against it, opposed tithing because of the financial hardship it placed upon them. Regardless of the reason for raising protests against tithing, the system estranged many people from the Church of England.

The antagonism of the laity is revealed in any one of a number of incidents. The tithe-payers used all their ingenuity to make things difficult for the tithe-owner. Millers tossed the handsful of meal out of their sacks, but would allow no boxes to be kept at hand in which this tithe might be gathered up for the parson. Dairymaids took their tithe-milk to church, and, if no one was there to receive it, they poured it out on the floor in front of the altar and departed. Discontented landowners put pressure on their tenants to leave the tithe sheaves badly bound so that they would fall to pieces on the way or rot in the rains.

The tithe wars were not confined to these irritating methods, since there were many cases where actual violence was used. Frequently, owners' servants, sent to collect the tithes, were set upon and severely assaulted, the corn trampled down, and the horses taken from the wagons and impounded. In the cities, men banded together to protest against—and resist payment of—this increasingly hateful tax. Many were arrested and imprisoned "for assembling of companyes to withstande the payment of their tythes." [24]

Contrary to the law,[25] many of the larger landowners went to the length of letting their tithable lands go derelict so that the tithe-owner should not get his tithe.[26] One Hampshire farmer duly notified the tithe-owner that he was about to draw a field of turnips. He waited until the men, carts, and horses were on the land, then pulled ten turnips, gave one to the men, and told them he would let the parson know when he planned to draw more.[27]

At the Sussex at Lewes, a case was considered in which a parson failed to come at once after being notified to take his tithe of lambs. It transpired that the farmer put his own nine lambs back with their mother, but was indifferent as to the fate of the tenth which he wished the tithe-owner to take away. The verdict went against the farmer, for the law read, "The time of the payment of Lambs, Kids, Calves, Pigs, &c. is regularly when they are so old, that they may be weaned and live without the Dam. . . ." [28]

The clergy had the law on their side! And they frequently found new ways to claim more tithes. To wit: a farmer was liable to tithe turnips. But, if he turned his sheep into the turnip field, he paid the tithe on the sheep, which made turnips exempt from the tithe. In one well-ordered farm, the farmer refrained from turning his flock into the entire field. Rather, he enclosed the flock in a portion of the field, picked the turnips in the remainder of the field, and threw them to the sheep! An ingenious Sussex clergyman considered that since these turnips were thrown to the sheep, he could claim tithe on the turnips. The claim was carried to the Court of Exchequer and decided by Lyndhurst in the clergyman's favor. The church thus won another technical victory and added one more claim to the intolerable exactions. But the claim, like many other claims of the church, was purchased dearly.[29]

Hostilities against the tithe system continued to mount. Farmers jeered the parsons and stoned auctioneers and bailiffs sent to collect the tithe or dispossess the landowners. In some cases, warlike barricades were thrown up, trenches dug across farm approaches, and gates buttressed with tree trunks. To sticks and

stones was added the protest of the old harvest song, sung by
the rebellious tillers:

> We've cheated the Parson;
>   We'll cheat him again.
> For why should a blockhead
>   Have one in ten
> For prating so long like a book-learned sot,
>   Till pudding and dumpling burn to pot? [30]

Another song, sung to the tune of Old Hundred, also voiced
the bitter protest:

> God save us from these raiding priests,
> Who seize our crops and steal our beasts,
> Who pray, "Give us our daily bread,"
> And take it from our mouths instead.[31]

It is no surprise that some clergymen gave up their livings rather
than collect the tithe by such legal means.[32]

Some of the dissenters paid heavily for their stand against the
tithe. A number of periodicals, published in England in the
eighteenth and nineteenth centuries, tell of the plight of the
Quakers. According to one such publication, at least 1180 persons had been persecuted in the Exchequer, ecclesiastical, and
other courts. Of this number, 302 suffered imprisonment and 9
died while in prison. The records show that one man, William
Francis of Luton, Bedfordshire, was confined in prison for nineteen months for the mere value of a groat. Two others, Ann and
Robert Henderson of Banton, Cumberland, were imprisoned
for eleven months for the failure to pay one penny.[33]

Men not only were fined and imprisoned for not paying
tithes, but were martyred for holding views which claimed doctrines of compulsory tithing to be contrary to the will of God.[34]

Apparently, the land as well as the people suffered under the
tithing system. One author, writing early in the nineteenth cen-

tury, pointed to the inability of improving barren land, because "ten per cent of its produce far exceeds the amount of any profit which can thereby be derived." [35] In some countries, farms were offered rent free, if the tenant would pay the tithe. In one case, a maiden lady had to expend capital on a farm before she could let it rent free, and, further, had to pay the tithe out of her own pocket! Some estates were cultivated for the benefit of the tithe-owner, alone.[36]

In 1836, an Act of Parliament ended the system of payment in kind, which was suited for a primitive, rural economy and substituted a money payment based on the prices of cereals. The clergy lost as much as 30 per cent of their income.[37] The Tithe Act of 1891 placed the responsibility of payment on the landlord. The permanent stabilization of the tithe and its collection by Queen Anne's Bounty came through the Act of 1925, but it did not bring peace.

At this point, the German system of *Kirchensteur* deserves mention. Writing in 1931, Willoughby Dewar stated that in every state of Germany all the more important religious denominations have been recognized officially as corporations with power to impose a levy on their members. The sums levied are collected by the ordinary revenue officials. The amount demanded from each contributor is, roughly, a tenth of what he pays in income tax, the exact percentage being fixed annually by the various church authorities, according to their alleged need. In Hamburg, the rate for Jews is 12 per cent, for Roman Catholics 8 per cent, and for Lutherans 7½ per cent.[38] The membership in these various denominations is voluntary, and the rate is kept as low as possible. If wealthy converts are taxed too heavily, they can change their membership.

In examining the growth and development of the tithe system to the Reformation Period, it is clear that certain basic New Testament principles were not observed.

After seeing the deplorable way in which the church exacted tithes—either by law or threats of excommunication—and after sensing the attitude of the laity toward the tithing system in post-Reformation England, it is not difficult to understand why tithing seldom was advocated in the early American church.

Church Rates

A second method of financing the church immediately after the Reformation was known as church rates. Tithes and church rates belong in somewhat the same category. The church rate was a tax imposed upon all people for upholding "the performance of divine service and for upholding the fabric." [39] In Scotland, some contended there was really no difference between the tithe and the church rate; both rested on the law of the land and on no other foundation.[40]

The history of this tax can be stated briefly. Offerings and tithes of the early church were distributed according to a fourfold division: one for the use of bishops, another for maintaining the fabric of the church (upkeep of the church property), a third for the poor, and a fourth to provide for the incumbent (resident pastor). As the years passed, the clergy more and more regarded tithes as their rightful property. This left the care of church property—the fabric—without support. Gradually, this burden was shifted to the parishioners whose contributions were, at first, purely voluntary. However, what began as a voluntary offering soon became a compulsory tax, known as the church rate.

Following the Reformation, much of the church property was in need of repairs. People were asked to help and, if they refused, they were put into the High Commission Court. This continued until the time of Charles II, under whom there was passed a series of litigations. Then, under William III, every individual was *"ex necessitate* a member of the existing church, and no man living dare disavow himself so to be." [41] Hence, the church rate was imposed on all citizens alike.

The Liberation Society published and circulated the "Church Rate Catechism," which carried a protest in the definition of the church rate. "The church rate is a tax levied on all the ratepayers of a parish for the repairs, and other expenses, of the place of worship frequented by the members of one religious denomination." [42] Those who imposed the tax preferred to think of it as a voluntary contribution. Like other taxes, however, it was voluntary only until the payment of it was refused. [43]

Each year, when the church rate was decided, the church was the scene of a bitter battle. The following song, printed by the Liberation Society, illustrates the tension that existed:

> Then came two days of agitation,
> Anger, scorn, and intimidation;
> The church was the scene of this holy war,
> Where the rector sat to lay down the law,
> As the close drew near, amid the din,
> Bets were laid as to who would win;
> When at six o'clock, a loud "Hoo-ray,"
> Proclaimed that "the Church had won the day." [44]

The dissenters, especially the Quakers, refused to pay the tax, and many of them endured much hardship rather than compromise. One man remained a prisoner in the jail for two years rather than pay the church rate assessed him. [45] Often, the dissenter's property was sold at auction to pay the rate due. A local paper pictured what happened at Neath:

> On this, as on previous occasions, porters were hired; but they evidently did their work more reluctantly. The tropies borne off from Mr. Ree's dwelling were four arm-chairs. These the porters carried for some distance, amidst the gibes and hootings of the crowd, accompa-

> nied by the firing-off of pistols and small
> guns. On reaching the market gates, the porters
> fairly abandoned their load in pure disgust.
> At least half an hour now elapsed before the
> police could find any party to convey the
> seized goods to their destination. They must be
> sold by auction; but the difficulty will be to find an
> auctioneer, as we have been informed that more
> than "one man of business" in that line has posi-
> tively refused to have anything to do with the
> matter.[46]

Sometimes the police had to carry out the confiscated goods. The law gave its officers power to enter a house and take suffi- cient goods that when they were sold at auction, would bring enough money to defray the unpaid rate and expenses. If the first room the police entered contained enough to satisfy their claim, they were obliged to take what was there and were not allowed to go farther. It was common for one nonconformist to go ahead of the police and give warning that they were on their way. One handy man went ahead of the police, offering to fix broken or discarded furniture that might be placed in the first room.

The police did not enjoy their task and were very apologetic as they entered the house, saying, for example, "Good morning, madam. Most unpleasant business this. Most unpleasant duty for me. If I had my own way, I'd rather be a hundred miles away; but duty is duty, and must be done. . . ." [47]

The "Church Rate Catechism" stated, "It is the most un- popular tax in England; the only one, in fact, that is resisted." [48] A Dr. Lushington is quoted as saying the church rate "created more feuds than any other subject I know." [49] Church rates were enforced by "summonses and distress warrants; by ex- pensive litigation in ecclesiastical courts; by means of magis- trates, policemen, brokers, and auctioneers; by taking men's

Bibles and beds, their silver spoons, and even their cooking utensils." [50]

The church rate was not a heavy tax. The objection to it was not based on the rate, but upon the principle that no man should be forced to pay for the support of another's religion.

Quakers and Baptists—who led the opposition—paid heavily for their stand, but victory was theirs, since the dissenters eventually were relieved of the church rate. In the process, the Church of England created enemies and estranged many from the church.

State Support

Political and social conditions in Europe discouraged the Reformers from carrying out the principles of individual freedom inherent in their doctrines. In instructing the evangelical groups to prepare for the Second Advent, Luther encouraged an organization based on the principle of financial self-support with freedom to call their own pastors.[51] However, the political philosophy and the unrest of the common people caused Luther to look to the secular powers to provide the necessary compulsion in church support.

At the Diet of Augsburg, 1555, the Lutheran faith was legalized and placed under the protection of the Lutheran princes. Evangelical ministers continued to receive the parsonages, glebe incomes, stipends, and fees. The Elector of Saxony, for instance, refused to take any of the confiscated convent lands and possessions for civil purposes; these, together with the church endowments, provided stipends for the pastors, salaries for the schoolmasters, and a settled provision for the poor.[52]

In fact, all plans of ecclesiastical government proceeded on the basis that the right of ecclesiastical oversight belonged to the supreme territorial secular authority. These plans—included within the one set of ordinances—gave provisions for the support of the ministry, for the maintenance of schools, and for the care of the poor.

Throughout Europe, where the Lutheran or Reformed churches were recognized, the ecclesiastical property of the medieval church, generally, was used for evangelical purposes. A case in point occurred in 1528 when the preachers of Aigle, Switzerland—Farel and Simon—were granted either "two hundred florins of Savory annually, and a house with a court, and a kitchen garden," or, if they preferred, they could have the old revenues of the parish curés. The pastors preferred to take the place of the Romanist incumbents. The history of Aigle was repeated over and over again in other parts of western Switzerland.[53]

When Gustaf Ericsson, commonly known as Gustaf Vasa, came to the throne in 1523, the church owned two-thirds of the land of Sweden, and the land owned by the church had been tax free. Therefore, the king planned to overthrow the ecclesiastical aristocracy by the help of the Lutheran Reformation. At the Diet of Westeras, 1527, the property of the church and the authority to regulate ecclesiastical affairs were delivered into the hand of King Gustavus. But the churches embracing the Protestant faith preserved their revenues.[54]

Although the methods of church support were not uniform throughout the Lutheran and Reformed churches, they were based, generally, on an intimate union of church and state. Specific methods of raising the money were revenues, tithes, endowments, and taxations; but the secular ruler provided the necessary compulsion by which the funds were collected.

In general, the Protestant mind clung to the idea that an intimate union of church and state was necessary to the purity of religion and good government. Those who broke with this theory were the groups known as Anabaptists, Quakers, Brownists, and Separatists. They believed in complete separation of church and state and in the voluntary principle of church support. These views, which began to ferment in this post-Reformation period, were held by the Pilgrims who settled Plymouth in 1620; consequently, this minority had some effect on the early church in America.

However, as the church moved to America, the general feeling, held by a majority of the immigrants, was in favor of state aid, because of their background in Europe and the church's slowness in recognizing all the implications of the Reformation emphasis on freedom and voluntary allegiance.

part *TWO*

MONEY AND THE CHURCH
IN EARLY AMERICA

VI.   Philosophies of Voluntary Support
      On the congregational level
      On the national level

VII.   Philosophies of Compulsory Support
      On the town level
      By the authority of the patroon
      By the authority of the colony and the king

VIII.   Methods of Support
      Glebes
      Pew revenues
      Collections and offerings
      Subscription lists
      Lotteries

VI

Philosophies of
Voluntary Support

In the colonies and on the American frontier two broad philosophies of church support were prevalent—namely, voluntary and compulsory—with numerous variations finding expression in these two streams of church support.

As could be expected, the backgrounds of the early settlers influenced their church life in the New World. The founding fathers of America did not all react in the same way to the conditions under which they had lived. Some desired to throw off the yoke of the Church of England; others wished to retain their fellowship with the Church of England but were indifferent to the claims of the king. Most of the colonists, however, were in hearty sympathy with the principle of an established church. Although some had suffered because of this principle, they generally agreed that their suffering was a consequence of a wicked application of the principle and not because it was inherently wrong.

Although one cannot classify the early American fathers in their attitudes toward church and state relationships in rigid categories, it is possible to note three general classifications. The first group was composed of the New England Puritans who established their congregational churches by law. The second group was the Anglicans who also established their churches by law in Virginia, Maryland, the Carolinas, Georgia, and to a

85

degree in limited areas of New York. The third group comprised those colonies in which there never was an establishment: Rhode Island, Pennsylvania, New Jersey, and Delaware.

There was also a variation in the geographical limits within which these various ideas or relationships were carried out. Some extended only to the congregation, others reached to the limits of town or patroon, and others embraced the entire colony.

This chapter will deal with the philosophies of voluntary support, and the next chapter will concern itself with the compulsory philosophy of church support.

On the Congregational Level

The philosophy of voluntary support on the congregational level was introduced in America by a group of Separatists from England. They clashed with the Church of England at two points—first, they adhered to Calvinistic principles; and, second, they objected to the Episcopal jurisdiction and discipline of the Church of England. From the small village of Scrooby, England, they migrated to the Netherlands. Nationalistic conflicts there caused dissatisfaction and led them to embark—after overcoming many barriers—for America. As every schoolboy knows, they landed on December 21, 1620, at the place where they established their colony, named Plymouth.

Considering their treatment at the hands of the Church of England, it is not surprising that they sought a new answer to the problem of church support. When they turned to the Bible, they found authority to support their various methods. The old Testament appeared to authorize tithes legally enforced. On the other hand, the New Testament was quoted as putting an end to the whole Jewish system, tithes included. Thus, the financial basis upon which the so-called "Brownist" or Separatist churches was founded was "That Ministers should onley live of volun-

tarie contributions & not either of set stipends or tithes." [1] John
Smyth, one of the Separatists, is quoted as saying:

> Wee hold that tithes are either Jewish or popish
> . . . that the officers of the Church in the necessity
> of the Church ought to work for their living, as
> Paul made tents. That the officers of the Church
> may challendg mayntenance of the Church, if the
> Church be able to yeeld it. That also the poore of
> the Church may require mayntenance uppon the
> same grounds, for we are al members one of
> another, & have al things common in use, though
> not in possession. [2]

John Robinson, who had at one time been the minister of the
group who came to Plymouth, wrote a book in 1610, entitled,
A Justification of Separation from the Church of England, in
which he stated,

> We do willingly leave unto you both your priestly
> order and maintenance, contenting ourselves with the
> people's voluntary contribution, whether it be less or
> more, as the blessing of God upon our labor, the fruit
> of our ministry, and a declaration of their love and
> duty. [3]

In 1608, this group had spent some time in Amsterdam—before going on to Leyden—from which they embarked for America. It is possible that the English Baptists, who also retreated
to Amsterdam, helped to deepen the Puritans' concern for religious freedom. The theory which the Separatists held regarding church support had been expressed as early as 1603 in the
"Points of Difference." The Amsterdam exiles criticized the
Church of England, saying the "due maintenance" of ministers
"should be of the free and voluntarie contribution of the
Church." [4] Also, in 1611, the English Baptists at Amsterdam

made it an article of faith that "The magistrate is not to meddle with religion or matters of conscience, not compel men to this or that form of religion; because Christ is the King and Lawgiver of the Church and conscience." [5]

The Plymouth colony included representatives of such ideas as these. It is significant, therefore, that for two generations they held as their ideal the principle of voluntary offerings. John Winthrop (1588-1649), the first governor of the Massachusetts Bay Colony,[6] indicates in his Journal that a weekly offering seems to have been part of the regular Sunday service at Plymouth. In the account of his visit to Plymouth in 1632, this sentence appears: "The deacon, Mr. Fuller, put the congregation in mind of their duty of contribution; whereupon the Governour and all the rest went down to the deacon's seat and put into the box and then returned." [7]

The Puritans who landed at Massachusetts Bay, 1630, for the most part were Independents, or Non-Separatist Congregationalists. They did not wish to separate themselves from the Church of England, but they did come to America with leanings toward the ideal of voluntary support. The Puritan theory was that all who entered the covenant would do so voluntarily and would voluntarily support the church. Yet, under the law it was expected that all people would contribute to the church.

The case of Thomas Goodwin was typical of many who—for conscience's sake—relinquished their legal rights of support to serve on the basis of voluntary offerings. Goodwin, of Christ's College and Catherine Hall, Cambridge, was chosen lecturer at Trinity Church, Cambridge, but in 1634 left his position—motivated by conscience—and in 1639 retired to Holland to become pastor of the English church at Arnhem. Regarding the support of the ministry, he said, "The contribution of maintenance to a minister is left free, and it is fit it should be so." In this way ". . . it may be an exercise of grace to the people, and an offering of sacrifice to God." He stated further:

> This act is left to the freedom of the people,
> that they may have an opportunity of exercising
> their love, to the increase of the grace of love in
> them. Whilst the minister enlargeth their hearts
> they stretch their purses for him.[8]

The Puritans carried convictions like this into the New World. Several sources give accounts of the way in which the voluntary gifts were received in the First Church of Boston. The deacons were in charge of the offering, and the people brought their gifts forward to the money box.

In strengthening the case for voluntary giving, Governor Winthrop set forth the position of John Cotton:

> After much deliberation and serious advice,
> the Lord directed the teacher, Mr. Cotton, to
> make it clear by the Scripture that the minister's
> maintenance, as well as all other charges of the
> church, should be defrayed out of a stock or
> treasury, which was to be raised out of the
> weekly contribution. Which accordingly was agreed
> upon. . . . Mr. Cotton preaching out of the 8 of
> Kings, 8, taught that when magistrates are forced
> to provide for the maintenance of ministers, etc.,
> then the churches are in a declining condition.
> Then they showed that the minister's maintenance
> should be by voluntary contribution, not by lands
> or revenues or tithes, etc., for these have always
> been accomplished with pride, contention, and
> sloth. . . .[9]

Thomas Hooker, who landed in Massachusetts in 1633 with some of his former parishioners and who later settled in Newton (Cambridge) as pastor, believed that ministerial support should be voluntary. However, he was not in favor of such complete liberty that might allow one to neglect his responsibility at this point. "The church," he said, "must make provision *not of liberty* or *courtesy,* which may be done or left undone; but it is a *duty* and a *work of justice* unto which the church is called, and to the performance whereof they are bound." He concluded his instruction by saying:

> In case any member shall fail in this contribution, he sins in a breach of the known rule of the gospel. It appertains to the church, to see the reformation of that evil; those who neglect this duty must be admonished by the deacons.[10]

Thus, even though the deacons were to admonish those who neglected their contributions, the contributions were, nevertheless, voluntary.

The evidence indicates the New England fathers came to America with the ideal of voluntary support. This ideal was manifested in the religious life of both the Pilgrims of Plymouth and the Puritans of Massachusetts Bay. However, the evidence points to the fact that the ideal of voluntary support was not translated into practice. The Puritans and the Pilgrims who made up the membership of the New England churches generally turned to taxation as the method of support.

Certain individual Puritans did, however, remain true to their convictions for separation of church and state. For instance, Roger Williams stood so firmly for the principle of voluntary support that he declined a call to the Boston Church because the church paid a stated salary. Because of his liberal views and his insistence that conscience cannot be controlled by civil power, he was banished from the colony. Accompanied by four others, he made a settlement (1636) on Narragansett Bay, calling it Providence. The government was planned as a pure democracy. His views on voluntary weekly offerings are expressed clearly:

> As to the laborer worthy of his reward, I answer,
> we find no other patterne in the Testament of Christ
> Jesus, but that both the converting (or Apostolicall
> Ministry) and the Feeding (or Pastorall Ministry)
> did freely serve or minister; and yet were freely
> supported by the Saints and Churches, and that not
> in stinted wages, tithes, stipends, sallaries, etc., but
> with larger or lesser supplies as the hand of the Lord
> was more or lesse extended in his weekly blessings
> on them.[11]

The statement above indicates the philosophy which the early American Baptists held, namely, free-will support—but not salaries, wages, stipends, or tithes. They denounced salary-paid ministers as "hirelings." Yet, the Baptist ministers did accept support from their congregations, and they were not always consistent in carrying out their philosophy of nonpaid ministry. To wit—an early Baptist minister in Alton, New Hampshire, preached against receiving money for preaching, but when he visited, he always carried his saddle bags with him and expected people to pay him "in kind." A few years later, this same man received a call to a church that offered a stated stipend, which he accepted at once.[12]

By and large, the Baptists—although inconsistent at times—remained true to the principles of separation of church and state and voluntary support of the ministry. They, more than any other group, are the representatives of the philosophy of church support which emphasizes voluntary support on the congregational level.

On the National Level

The philosophy of voluntary support in the early American period also expressed itself on a national level in Methodism. It was a unique adventure.

The world was Methodism's parish. Her preachers were sent wherever there was a need. Her ideal was an equalization of salaries for all preachers, regardless of the area in which they might serve or the amount of money that might be raised on their respective circuits. The support of the ministry was completely voluntary. In fact, for a time, offerings were received only among the members of the societies (local churches); visitors were not given an opportunity to contribute. To carry out Methodism's ideal of a boundless ministry, the ministers were supported, not on the congregational level or the circuit level, but on a national level. The plan required ministers' salaries to be limited to a certain figure, and in a given circuit all support in money or in kind—above the stated salary—was to be used to supplement the salaries of ministers whose circuits were unable to raise the full amount. There was never a contract between the people and their preachers. In addition, the early records of Methodism stipulated that a minister who received a salary on the basis of a subscription list would be dismissed from the ministry.

Before discussing Methodism's attempt at national support, a glance at John Wesley's view of the Christian's use of money will prove enlightening.

In his famous sermon on "The Use of Money," [13] he reduced his instructions to three plain rules: "Gain all you can, save all you can, give all you can." Under the first heading he enlarged on principles to be followed in gaining all one can. These principles can be summed up in the thought that one never must gain by exploiting either himself or others in mind, soul, or body. The second admonition is to be carried out by spending money for essential things, only. Resources and talents are not to be wasted in gratifying the flesh either by excessive spending on one's self or by giving it to children who know not the value thereof.

The Methodists followed quite well these admonitions, being industrious and able to gain much. They were frugal and saved much that they had gained. But they misinterpreted the primary purpose for which they were to save, namely, that they might give as much as possible.

Wesley, commenting on gaining and saving, observes, "All this is nothing, if a man not go forward, if he does not point all this at a farther end." Apparently, the people thought then—as they do now—that "saving all you can" meant to put it in the bank! But Wesley insisted, "You may as well throw your money into the sea, as bury it in the earth. And you may as well bury it in the earth, as in your chest, or in the Bank of England." [14]

In another sermon—entitled "The Good Steward"—he left no doubt in the minds of his hearers or readers that man, being a steward, has no right to dispose of anything he has, but according to the will of God.[15]

Speaking of sanctification, in a letter to John Newton, April 1, 1766, Wesley said, "In food, apparel, and all things else, I advise all those under my care to save all they can (with a safe conscience) in order to give all they can." [16]

Further evidence of this conviction is brought out in his sermon "On Dress." [17] He condemned costly dress simply because it takes money that otherwise would be available for the naked, the hungry, and the strangers. "Every Shilling which you needlessly spend on your apparel is, in effect, stolen from God and the poor." [18]

To the man who says he can *afford* extravagance, Wesley answered, "No man living can *afford* to waste part of what God has committed to his trust." [19] Nor did he allow his hearers to think these words applied only to those with an abundance of money. In his sermons "On Riches" [20] and "On the Danger of Increasing Riches," [21] he included all who have food to eat and raiment to put on, with something over, as being rich.

Wesley propounded a doctrine of stewardship that, if carried out, would have brought forth an abundance of financial resources for the work. But, as we shall see in the remainder of this chapter, few were willing to accept Wesley's discipline of stewardship.

Methodism's first official statement regarding voluntary national support for ministers is found in the *Minutes of the Second Conference of the Methodist Societies,* May 17, 1775. It read, "Every preacher to be allowed six pounds, Pennsylvania currency, per quarter, and his travelling charges besides." [22] Accordingly, the annual allowance would be 24 pounds in Pennsylvania currency, or approximately $64.

In 1778, the salary question was raised again, and it was decided that the quarterage—the support per quarter—should be eight pounds, Virginia currency.[23] It was also decided that an equal amount was to be allowed for the wives of married preachers. The records show, however, that funds were not available to pay even the preachers, to say nothing about payment for the wives!

By 1783, eleven preachers' wives were named for whom provision was to be made; it was proposed to raise 260 pounds to meet this need. The following year the names of the wives needing provision were listed in the *Minutes,* with various amounts apportioned to the different societies, to be raised in order to meet the needed sum.

Bishop Asbury, as well as other leaders in the early Methodist Church, desired to see the ministers remain single, hence the Conference was reluctant in granting the wives allowances, especially when the preachers themselves were not receiving the stated salary in full.

The ideal of equal support for all preachers seems to have been carried out even to include support in kind. For example, in 1782, the Conference directed the stewards and preachers to evaluate the clothing donated, and to report it as part of the salary. The steward's record for a circuit in Indiana, in 1820, shows a variety of goods received toward the preacher's support—bridle leather, shoe leather, corn, linen, shoes, and a pair of socks.[24]

The "Christmas Conference," as the organizing body of American Methodism has been called, held in Baltimore, 1784, fixed the annual salaries at twenty-four pounds, Pennsylvania currency, "and no more." [25] The added words, "and no more," leads one to believe some preachers may have been receiving more than the stated amount. This conference, again, gave the wives an equal amount, "if they need it," and it allowed additional amounts for the preachers' children. For each child under the age of six years, an amount of six pounds was allowed; and for each child between six and eleven years of age, an additional eight pounds was allowed. These allowances for children, however, were challenged in 1787, for a number of preachers still were not receiving their salaries in full. Thus, it was ruled that "for the future, no married preacher shall demand more than 48, P.C." (Pennsylvania Currency).[26]

The following year, 1788, many preachers again failed to receive their full salaries. The Conference, once more, tried to persuade the preachers to report all support, provisions as well as money, in order that all salaries might be brought up to the agreed-upon figure.[27] Nevertheless, records for the following year, 1790, show that the deficiencies of the preachers' salaries amounted to more than 1,071 pounds, and that the total amount available to meet these deficiencies was less than 122 pounds. Since the brethren in Kentucky, Ohio, and the extremities of the states of New York and Connecticut were in greatest need, the 122 pounds were divided among them, "the whole to be sent in books." [28]

In July, 1785, Congress adopted a resolution making the dollar the money unit of the United States of America. For the next few years there was financial unrest, and many ministers underwent tremendous hardships due to the fluctuation of state and local currency. In 1792, the action of the Methodist Church adopted the dollar as legal tender for ministers' salaries, and the salary set at $64 and traveling expenses.[29] In 1796 the allowance to a preacher's wife was made without the condition, "if she want it," or "if she be in need of it." Wives could now make claims on the funds on the same basis as their husbands.[30]

The General Conference of 1800 legislated a substantial increase in salaries and allowances when it set the salary at $80 plus traveling expenses. An equal amount was allowed for the preacher's wife, and additional amounts were allowed for the children of the parsonage. Each child to the age of seven years was allowed $16 annually, and each child between seven and fourteen years of age was allowed $24. An allowance of $80 was provided for "superannuated, worn-out, and supernumerary preachers," and for the wives of "superannuated, worn-out, and supernumerary preachers." Likewise, the orphans of preachers were allowed $16 annually.[31]

Between 1800 and 1816, only two minor changes were made concerning salary scales—an increase in the allowance for orphans and an allowance for preachers who were not full members of an annual conference, known as "local" preachers.

In 1816, the General Conference of the Methodist Episcopal Church enacted a stated salary and allowances for the last time; it was $100 for all preachers and an equal amount for their wives. The allowances for children continued to be the amount set in 1800. An additional allowance was made for fuel, table expenses, and heavy furniture for the home.

A completely different philosophy of ministerial support was acted upon in 1860 by the General Conference. The *Discipline* of the Methodist Episcopal Church of that year directed the churches or circuits to furnish a comfortable support to the preachers, taking into consideration the number and condition of the family, traveling expenses, and moving expenses. In short, the ideal of a uniform support was no longer official!

Was Methodism's ideal of uniform salaries ever realized? No. The dream was there, but it never came true. Previous to the year 1800, funds were never adequate to bring all salaries up to the stated figure of $64. A few men may have failed to report all they had received in the course of the year; some may have failed to turn in to the Conference all that was in excess of the approved figure. In any event, the stewards—who were in charge of the finances—reported all income, but the surpluses were not sufficient to bring all salaries to the agreed-upon salary. What surpluses were available were distributed according to the greatest need, but there still remained a wide discrepancy.

The ideal of uniform salaries not only failed to be realized before 1800, but, in a sense, the year 1800 marks the beginning of a forsaking of the ideal. That year the rule requiring a report of all gifts and donations by friends was repealed. This rule did not, however, cover wedding fees, since they were to be turned in to the Conference.[32]

A move—instigated by Dr. Coke—was also under way urging the circuits to provide parsonages.[33] Children were being included as claimants, and the amounts allowed to them were designated. Obviously, a man with a family, serving a circuit which had accepted Dr. Coke's recommendation to provide a parsonage, and receiving donations of food and clothing from the members, had a considerably larger salary than a single man who may have served a group whose generosity had not been so well developed.

Another stumbling block in the uniform salary endeavor was the support of the bishops. Theoretically, their salaries were the same as those allowed to preachers. But they were never at the mercy of an individual circuit as were the preachers. Prior to 1800, the bishops received their support largely from private friends, with any deficit being made up by particular societies.[34] All cash which the bishops received—above $64—was to be turned in to the Conference.[35] But no limitation was put on what they might receive from friends—Asbury was given a four-wheeled carriage by Philadelphia friends [36]; to McKendree was bequeathed as much as $2,000 by some friends who died child-less.[37] In both cases, these men used their gifts for the work; nevertheless, it is obvious their support was not on an equal basis with other preachers.

Finally, the dream of a unified salary began to fade in the early 1800's when men in the cities and larger churches accepted increases in salaries and failed to turn in to the Conference those funds in excess of the disciplinary figure. A series of articles on Methodism, in 1834, revealed some of the larger salaries of Methodist ministers which had been paid in the year 1821, just five years after the General Conference had set the salary at $100. Several examples were a Mr. Hunt who received $750 plus house rent; a Mr. Merwin who received $847; a Mr. Hib-bard, $763; and a Mr. Spicer, $564.[38]

Further evidence of the fading of Methodism's dream is given in an account of a trial for libel in New York, brought by Azor Hoyt against a group of Methodist ministers. The allowance at that time, 1840, for a married man was still $200 plus table ex-pense, parsonage, travel expense, and an allowance for children. According to the regulations, all money received for ministerial support by a church or circuit over $200 plus the specified allowances was to be turned in to the Conference to supplement salaries below the $200 figure. At the trial, however, Dr. Dur-bin, a Methodist minister testified:

> My salary is twelve hundred and fifty dollars annu-
> ally; that of Mr. Bangs, I think, fifteen hundred or

upward—that of Mr. Merritt, about twelve hundred
—that of Mr. Waugh, sixteen hundred—that of
Mr. Mason is, I think, over one thousand and under
fifteen hundred dollars.[39]

To compare the salaries above with the average salaries of
Methodist ministers throughout the church, the figures from the
Minutes of the 1844 annual conference are compiled in the
following table.[40] Opposite the annual conferences, the first
column indicates the amount of money necessary to bring all
salaries up to the authorized figure of $200 for a married
preacher—plus allowances for children—and $100 for each un-
married man. The second column shows the amount actually
brought to the annual conference to make up the deficits. The
third column indicates the average amount on the dollar that
the preachers received who reported deficits. The minutes failed
to give the number of men who reported deficits.

Methodism's emphasis resulted in a burden-bearing ministry,
but not a burden-bearing laity!

Francis Asbury often spoke of his "poor and destitute
preachers," or "poor and suffering preachers." They were poor
and destitute because early Methodism's vision of stewardship
was not equal to the vision of her missionary ministry. This
fact is summed up in the words of Harvey Reeves Calkins, one
of the outstanding leaders in the field of church finance in the
last generation:

> . . . the exalted dispensation of the gospel,
> which was committed to the Methodists, de-
> manded an equally exalted program of steward-
> ship, and herein their failure in those
> momentous days of the beginning proved nothing
> less than a calamity.[41]

No man was more willing to endure the poverty and hardships of the itinerancy than Bishop Asbury. As he and Mc-

TOTAL SALARY DEFICIENCIES, TOTAL FUNDS AVAILABLE FOR DEFICIENCIES, AND AVERAGE CENTS ON THE DOLLAR PAID TO CLAIMANTS IN THIRTY ANNUAL CONFERENCES IN 1844 *

Annual Conference	Total Deficiency	Funds Available	Cents Paid on Dollar
Georgia	$ 6,697.23	$ 2,565.30	.38
South Carolina	3,408.55	2,105.67	.62
Baltimore	10,427.48	3,679.05	.35
Philadelphia	4,946.04	4,353.66	.88
New Jersey	3,331.00	3,056.00	.92
New York	8,856.00	4,572.94	.51
Troy	12,941.85	1,601.39	.12
Providence	3,221.00	1,040.00	.32
New Hampshire	1,348.80	1,104.39	.82
Pittsburgh	8,643.00	1,682.73	.19
New England	(No record)		
Erie	9,794.27	1,413.57	.14
Black River	3,386.33	1,445.24	.43
Rock River	10,086.38	1,148.11	.11
Maine	14,934.55	1,197.92	.08
North Ohio	3,527.76	1,396.17	.39
Iowa	2,945.34	1,012.00	.34
Oneida	10,842.87	1,856.31	.17
Illinois	9,811.80	1,221.26	.13
Ohio	8,137.60	1,740.39	.21
Genesee	17,744.00	1,325.21	.07
Kentucky	10,587.64	1,683.33	.16
Indiana	8,070.00	1,252.14	.15
Missouri	(No record)	1,356.34 †	
Michigan	8,283.99	1,206.01	.15
Holston	4,125.71	1,107.00	.27
North Indiana	8,617.94	1,207.60	.14
Tennessee	4,396.65	1,510.04	.34
Virginia	6,506.72	2,173.59	.33
Arkansas	3,628.07	1,167.76	.32
Memphis	3,831.11	1,455.49	.38
North Carolina	(No record)	1,316.75 †	
Mississippi	5,529.00	1,636.20	.30
Totals	$218,608.68	$53,916.47 **	

* Compiled from *Minutes*, III, 430-550.
** This total does not include the amounts reported by the Missouri †
and North Carolina † conferences because they failed to report the total
deficiencies which would be necessary for a true picture.

Kendree were on their way to an annual conference in 1808, he wrote in his Journal:

> My flesh sinks under labor. We are riding
> in a poor thirty dollar chaise, in partnership,
> two bishops of us, but it must be confessed that
> it tallies well with the weight of our purses.
> What bishops! Well—but we have great news,
> and we have great times, and each western,
> southern, and the Virginia conference will
> have one thousand souls truly converted to God.
> Is not this an equivalent for a light purse?
> And are we not well paid for starving and toil?
> Yes, glory to God! [42]

Volumes have been written of the labors and personal sacrifices of Francis Asbury. Yet, a church historian who served with Asbury on the early circuits, attributed much of the poverty in the ministry to the emphasis of this second bishop of the Methodist Episcopal Church.

According to Nathan Bangs, there were two defects in Asbury's administration. The first defect was a forsaking of the educational program of the church after two disheartening fires destroyed the two colleges started by the administration. The second defect was a reluctance in encouraging the people to support their ministers in a proper manner.[43]

Bangs tells of a certain steward of a circuit who, when urged to exert himself to make a more ample provision for the support of the preachers, remarked that he had heard Bishop Asbury pray to the Lord to keep the preachers poor! The presiding elder, to whom this remark was made, replied, "Such a prayer in that place was quite unnecessary, as he [the steward] and the people would, without any prompting, see that this was done to perfection." [44]

In their notes on the *Discipline,* Coke and Asbury write,

"Lovers of earthly riches will not long remain traveling preachers." [45] Apparently, Asbury felt poverty and suffering would assure zeal and sincerity. He labored to raise money for the support of the preachers, literally begging from door to door. But his emphasis was on a distorted conception of "mite-giving" [46] rather than on generosity and complete stewardship. Wherever he went, he carried his list of "mite" subscribers and worked diligently to get more people to pledge or subscribe toward the support of the "poor and suffering" preachers. He often recorded in his Journal, "I preached . . . we collected liberally on the mite subscription to help the suffering ministry." [47] One of the last requests which Bishop Asbury made before he died was for Mr. Bond to read the "mite subscription," which, incidentally, carried a maximum pledge of one dollar per person.[48]

The most disastrous result of this lack of stewardship motivation and education was the "locating" of men because of weakness of body or family concerns. The statistics of various records indicate that a number of men were taken from the traveling ministry because of their family requirements.

Asbury had a growing concern over the number of men who "located" (discontinued the active ministry) within a relatively few years after their admission. But he failed to see the problem as an economic condition. As he grew older, he feared "temporal prosperity for his preachers" and, above all, dreaded the marriage of the itinerants, which seemed to him "to menace almost fatally the whole ministry of Methodism in the new world." He was pleased to observe in the extreme South a prejudice in families against the marriage of their daughters with Methodist preachers, and says, "Thus involuntary celibacy is imposed upon us. All the better: Care and anxiety about worldly possessions do not stop us in our course. . . ." [49]

Ironically, Asbury's dream of a unified salary for all Methodist preachers became a dead issue, assisted by Asbury's own failure to understand stewardship. After the official action of 1860, which presented a completely different philosophy of ministerial support, the Methodist Church took her place alongside the other denominations, leaving ministerial support to congregational action.

VII

Philosophies of Compulsory Support

A second broad philosophy of church support in early America was compulsory support, expressed in at least three different ways: (1) on the town level, (2) by the authority of the patroon, and (3) by the authority of the colony and the king.

On the Town Level

Compulsory taxation, carried out on the town level, was a system inaugurated by New England congregationalism, motivated by the principles which the Puritans used in organizing themselves.

New England Puritanism. Like the Plymouth Pilgrims, the Puritans of Massachusetts Bay wished to purify the Church of England. Yet, upon landing in America, they set up a theocratic government which allowed less freedom to dissenters than had the Church of England. Church membership was made a basic requirement for franchise. Those who refused to conform to Puritan dogma were disciplined, banished, and, in extreme cases, put to death. The only freedom given to the Quakers, Baptists, and other dissenting groups was the freedom to stay away.

A Puritan state-church closely related to town government gradually developed to take the place of the Old Anglican state-church to which they had been accustomed in England. The meetinghouse was used for worship and for governmental purposes. In some cases, the minutes of the two organizations were kept in the same books. This close connection between church and state in Massachusetts began with the very first court, held on August 23, 1630, when it was ordered that ministers should be maintained at the public charge. This order was repeated and continued as the law of Massachusetts for more than two hundred years. At a General Court held at Boston, September 6, 1638, this matter was discussed, and action taken which allowed the town to assess each inhabitant; and, if a man did not pay his assessment "voluntarily," he would be compelled to pay it.[1]

Theoretically, the church was to be supported by voluntary contributions, but the court provided the necessary compulsion if the voluntary contributions were not forthcoming.

When the four congregational commonwealths entered into the union of 1643, one of the first acts of the commissioners was to recommend to the courts of Plymouth, Massachusetts, Connecticut, and New Haven the enactment of laws for church support. The first part of the recommendation suggested that each person be permitted to set down what he would be willing to pay. However, if a man was too conservative in his pledge, he was assessed by the town authority. Also, the assessment was to be collected by civil power if necessary.[2] This overture, which kept the appearance of being voluntary while rendering ministerial maintenance a public tax, was made a statute of Connecticut on October 25, 1644.

The Plymouth colony was more friendly to the idea of separation of church and state, but on June 5, 1655, it passed a mild enactment authorizing magistrates, in the case of obstinate neglecters, "to use such other meanes as may put them upon their duty." [3] The statutes of New Haven colony, printed in 1656, had a provision similar to that of Massachusetts.

Although some of the New England fathers may have given

up the ideal of voluntary support with reluctance, once they entered upon the road of legal prescription, more exacting laws soon followed. In November, 1647, the Massachusetts General Court authorized towns to levy taxes to supply their ministers with houses. The same body, in August, 1654, directed the county courts, upon complaint, to fix ministers' salaries and collect them by distraint. An official Connecticut report on the English authorities, in 1680, declared ministers' maintenance was "raysed upon the people by way of a rate," and a law of May, 1687, provided that salaries due from any town "shall be levied and assessed on the several inhabitants in each town or plantation according to their respective estates as from time to time they shall be in the genll [general] list," and collected "by such person or persons as the respective townes shall from year to year choose and appoint for that end." [4]

It is significant to note that for some reason the voluntary principle in church support was retained even into the period of taxation. The reason may have been practical, or it may have been due to religious convictions. Whatever the motive, the fact is that some churches, such as Boston, did not find it necessary to resort to the compulsory method entirely. As time passed and new sects began to be formed, there was a growing disinclination to be taxed arbitrarily for the support of the churches. For example, in the records of the earlier years of the parish in Jamaica Plain, founded in 1770, one reads of repeated annual votes to raise the expenses by a subscription rather than to be taxed upon the town valuation.

The success of the compulsory method in New England was due largely to the close relation between church and state. The congregation elected the minister, and the town paid his salary. Only so long as the most influential people of the community were members of the church did the compulsory method remain successful. Thomas Jefferson Wertenbaker points out that congregationalism, because of its emphasis upon localism, would have been hopelessly weak had it not enjoyed the full support of the civil authorities.[5]

Colonial Presbyterianism. Early Presbyterian churches followed a pattern similar to that of the congregational churches. The church at Jamaica provides an example of the way in which the town first assumed responsibility for the church. Early in the year 1662, the inhabitants of the town of Rustdrop, in the Dutch Province of New Netherland, voted to erect a house for their minister. This marked the beginning of the activities of the organization which today is known as the First Presbyterian Church of Jamaica, New York. The earliest record of the church appears in the minutes of a town meeting held on January 12, 1662, when it was decided to levy a special tax on real estate to meet the expenses of building a "minister's house." [6]

At this time, all churches on Long Island were town churches, erected and supported by the town. On February 14, 1663, it was voted to pay the pastor of the Jamaica church a salary of sixty pounds a year. This was to be paid in wheat at six shillings a bushel and Indian corn at three shillings and sixpence a bushel. The record states, "All the inhabitants of this town shall pay toward the maintenance of the ministry according to what they possess." [7]

The English took New Netherland on September 8, 1664, calling the colony New York. The Duke of York succeeded to the throne of England under the title of James the Second in 1685. And the next year he sent instructions to Governor Thomas Dongan to grant toleration to all Protestant sects, but to recognize the Church of England as the established church in the colony. Problems began to arise between reformed churches and the established church—the Church of England—soon after the Act for Settling the Ministry was passed September 22, 1693.

The act did not deny to any Protestants the right to worship as they chose, but it did compel non-Episcopalians in Jamaica and in the four counties of New York to pay a tax for the support of the Episcopal Church.

Not being certain whether a minister called by them could receive the tax money, the Presbyterians decided, on January 1, 1694, to pay their pastor, George Phillips, a salary of sixty pounds a year, to be raised by voluntary subscriptions.

On May 15, 1699, the colonial assembly passed a Building Act which permitted any town in the province to tax the freeholders in order to meet the expense of erecting a house of worship. Jamaica took advantage of the law and by the tax completed the church building. Some of the citizens refused to pay the tax, but arbitrators provided that those in arrears should pay the amount assessed or be forever acquitted of any further claim in connection with the edifice. The claims were met fully on April 28, 1701.

For the next thirty years, the question of title on the minister's house, church lands, and the stone church, as well as the question of the right of the government to tax all the inhabitants of the town for the support of the Episcopal ministry, caused a series of distractions and disturbances. All went comparatively well until a new governor, Lord Cornbury, arrived on the scene in 1702. He determined to give the tax money to the Church of England and to award the church property to the established church. Contrariwise, on October 29, 1724, the Supreme Court decided the case in favor of the Presbyterians, who thereafter enjoyed undisputed possession of the property. Not until 1753, however, were the properties actually given to the Presbyterians by the town.[8]

A second example which shows early Presbyterianism as a tax-supported institution is the First Presbyterian Church in Newark, New Jersey. Jonathan F. Stearns, author of a history of this congregation, states that the settlement of Newark in the years 1666 and 1667 was probably the last attempt to realize the noble dream of the old Puritan emigrants, namely, a church state. On October 30, 1666, forty settlers signed an agreement committing themselves to the "maintenance of the purity of religion professed in the Congregational churches." [9]

During the first seventy years, the town transacted all the business of the congregation. The first seven ministers were called to the office and had their salaries fixed by a vote of the town in the town meeting. The annual appropriations for the support of the ministers were made in the same way as other expenses of the town. Newark Church records reveal a lack of complete agreement in taxing each one for the minister's salary. One example is the action taken on January 2, 1687, indicating that the usual method of a church "rate" was set aside and the voluntary method was employed.[10]

Another approach was made the following year when it was agreed that the officials should "speak to the young men in our town that are for themselves, and see what they will voluntarily pay to the minister." [11] Ten years later, however, it was "agreed by vote that the town will raise 100 in a way of a rate for the upholding of the worship of God amongst us for a year." [12]

These records give evidence that the method of support was generally in the hands of church officials. And, if the church officials felt a public tax was necessary, they apparently had the power to impose such a tax.

Agitation for exemption from religious taxation commenced as soon as the number of dissenters began to increase. Presbyterianism, consequently, made a quiet transition from tax-support to the pew-rent system. The transition from tax-support to voluntary support in New England, on the other hand, involved more distress. In 1727, the Episcopalians in Massachusetts were allowed to pay their assessment to a clergyman of their faith, if there was an Episcopal minister in the town. Likewise, in Connecticut a similar relaxation took place, allowing Episcopalians to designate their tax to the Episcopal minister. During 1728-29 Massachusetts and Connecticut extended the same exemption to Quakers and Baptists.[18]

More liberal exemptions were allowed by Massachusetts in 1780 and by Connecticut in 1784. Both commonwealths still maintained the principle that all persons should be taxed for the support of religious institutions, and both recognized one standard polity and faith in each town. Those not of the recognized polity and faith were dissenters, who had to deposit with the town clerk a formal certificate in order to secure exemption. This system came to an end in Connecticut in 1818 and in Massachusetts in 1834.

When the revolt began to be launched against the established order, the clergy threw the full weight of their influence against the change. In their election sermons they lauded the established government as the best and purest in the world and the magistrates as godly men who had done nothing to merit "the murmurings of discontented people." [14] But the principles of the Reformation were being appreciated throughout the nation. For the first time since the Reformation, a nation was beginning to be formed which would allow religious freedom.

By the Authority of the Patroon

Another approach to church support in early America is seen in the records of New Netherland, an indefinite area in which the main settlement was New Amsterdam, later known as New York. The Dutch West India Company supported the first few ministers who were brought to New Netherland, but soon this responsibility was placed in the hands of proprietors, called "patroons." The patroons, in turn, compelled the people to bear the support of the church through taxes and assessments.

Although Henry Hudson (1609) and Adriaen Block (1610) were the first to establish a white settlement on Manhattan Island, it was the Dutch West India Company that named the post New Amsterdam and colonized it. The company made New Netherland a province in 1623, alliances were made with the Indians, and trade in peltry began at once. Peter Minuit, born in the city of Wesel of Huguenot parentage, was appointed Director of New Netherland by the West India Company, December 19, 1625, and he landed at New Amsterdam, May 4, 1626. Upon the arrival of Domine Jonas Michaelius, in April, 1628, Minuit and his brother-in-law, Huyghens, were chosen to be the ruling elders of the Dutch Church which Michaelius established.

In a letter, dated August 11, 1628, addressed to Reverend Adrian Smoutius, who was a minister of the Collegiate Churches of Amsterdam, Rev. Michaelius gave the first information concerning his financial support.[15] He revealed that the West India Company had assured him support, either by providing "free table" for him and his family or by giving him a few acres of land. He, however, had no means by which to farm, and his supply of food was quite limited, and he lacked the seewan (a whale fin or whale bone which was very useful in barter in those days) with which to buy from the Indians.

The system of patroonships was established by the West India Company in 1629, and placed the responsibility of ministerial support on the patroons or proprietors. The proprietors were ordered to ". . . exert themselves to find speedy means to maintain a clergyman and schoolmaster, in order that Divine Service and zeal for religion may be planted in that country. . . ." [16] The order did not specify the "means" by which the maintenance was to be provided, and it is not surprising that a variety of methods were attempted.

In Albany, for example, the patroon assumed responsibility for support for the first year only. The second year he withdrew his support altogether, and the congregation was required to raise the salary.

An interesting variation is seen in the arrangement made with the New Amsterdam officials. They were to be responsible for the ministers' salaries in return for the excise tax on rum and whisky. But, evidently, the officials of the town failed to keep their promise, since Stuyvesant had to remind them that they were allowed ". . . the Tavern keepers' Excise on the distinct promise, that your Worships would then provide means and take care, that the ministers of the Gospel should be paid their salaries." [17] They still did not carry out their promise, so the tavern keepers' excise was taken from these officials and let out to the highest bidder who would employ this tax in the support of the clergy.

The most common way by which the church was supported in New Amsterdam was by a public tax. This was the recommendation in the proposed Articles for Colonization and Trade of New Netherland in 1638.[18]

The contract between proprietor Van Rensselaer and the Reverend John Megapolensis illustrates the way in which a patroon called a minister to come to America to serve. This particular contract covered a period of six years. Mr. Megapolensis, his wife, and their four children were responsible for their clothing, furniture, and other utensils that could be stowed away properly in the ship. His salary was to commence as soon as he set foot on the colony; but, during the ocean trip across, the patroon was to provide free board for the family, and upon arrival the patroon was to pay at once three hundred guilders, without deduction.[19]

Apparently, the New Netherland system worked a hardship on the ministers, since the people did not support them willingly and the patroons found it difficult to enforce the various taxes. Many of the people had little interest in religion. Some gave the excuse that they were Catholics, or that they did not understand the Dutch language. Church members who came from the Old Country had not had the responsibility of supporting the church, as that had been done by the State.

Collecting the taxes was a problem. The court records of New Amsterdam contain two entries which reveal the employment of a collector, to be paid out of the money collected.[20]

A peaceful transition was made to British rule in 1664, but it brought financial hardship to the Dutch ministers. Governor Lovelace attempted various ways to provide for them. First, he directed, on June 28, 1670, that a levy was to be placed upon all inhabitants to provide the ministers with a yearly salary of 1,000 Dutch guilders, a rent-free dwelling, and free firewood.[21] Unfortunately, the new law did not move the people to give willingly.

Six months later, Governor Lovelace tried again by interceding and suggesting three ways to raise the money. The first was to make a custom charge of five per cent on imported rum and wines. The second was to place an imposition on rum and wines going to Albany. The third was to levy a general tax on nearby towns in place of the excise charge on rum and wines that was required at the time.[22] What would the preachers have done without the sale of rum and wines?

The Lutheran Church also had a problem supporting its pastors. For many years the West India Company successfully kept Lutheran pastors out of the colony. A letter of September 22, 1660, however, states "that the Lutherans are taking up subscriptions for the support of a Lutheran minister." [23] Yet, in 1674, the "Elders and Principals of the Augsburg Congregation" petitioned the governor to order the people of their confession (Lutheran) to pay what they promised on the minister's salary.[24]

Throughout the early days of the New Netherland's life the

responsibility of church support was handed down from the West India Company to the patroons, and from the patroons to town officials, who then placed a tax on the people. And, as could be expected, the people did not pay the tax willingly.

By the Authority of the Colony and the King

The fourth approach to church support in early America was compulsory support on the colonial basis. This philosophy was inspired directly by the Church of England, and it resulted in the establishment of Anglicanism in Virginia, in the Carolinas, and in New York.

Church Support in Anglican Virginia. The "Articles, Instructions, and Orders," dated November 20, 1606, and given to the London Company, which established the first permanent settlement in Virginia, gives a most significant pre-Puritan reference to the Christian purpose of American colonization:

> ... And wee doe specially ordaine, charge,
> and require, the said presidents and councells,
> and the ministers of the said several colonies
> respectively, within their several limits and
> precincts, that they, with all diligence, care,
> and respect, doe provide, that the true word,
> and service of God and Christian faith be
> preached. . . .[25]

On May 13, 1607, one hundred emigrants made the first permanent English settlement in America, naming it Jamestown in honor of James I. A month later, on June 21, 1607, a communion service was held there by a Church of England minister, Robert Hunt (1558-1608). The Reverend Mr. Hunt was chosen for the service by the Archbishop of Canterbury; and the London Company voted 500 pounds for his support.[26] The first representative government in the New World met at Jamestown in 1619, established the authority of the Church of England, and took measures for its support.[27]

Among the instructions to the governor was one providing for one hundred acres of land to be set aside toward the support of the several ministers in the colony, and that other provisions be made so as to make the living of every minister "two hundred pounds sterling or more." [28] The Virginia Assembly, in 1621-22, passed an enactment that each clergyman was to receive from his parishioners fifteen hundred pounds of tobacco and sixteen barrels of corn. This was the most anyone was compelled to pay, and every male of sixteen years and over was liable for assessment. If, however, this levy failed to produce the desired two hundred pounds, sterling, the minister was to be content with less.[29]

From the Acts of 1623 are preserved other decisions in regard to church support. The act provided penalties: for absence from church, a fine of five pounds of tobacco; for speaking "disparagingly of any minister without proof," a fine of five hundred pounds of tobacco. The assembly took other means for the support of the clergy, such as allowing glebes which were to be cultivated at the public expense.[30]

In 1629, the Assembly declared, ". . . it is thought fitt that all who works in the ground, of what qualitie, or condition soever, should pay tithes to the minister." Three years later, the Assembly ordered the minister's tobacco and corn to be deposited "in such place as he may appoynt, before any other tobacco of any man's cropp be disposed of"; also, "because of the low rate of tobacco," that there should be given to the minister "the 20th calfe, the 20th kidd of goates, and the 20th pigge." The minister's fees, called "petty duties," were fixed at two shillings for marrying, one shilling for churching, and one for burying. Christening was to be performed gratis. It was

ordered, also, that the church wardens should collect all ministerial dues and themselves be responsible on failures.[31]

The Assembly of March 1642-43 consolidated and unified
earlier enactments and created a comprehensive law which governed the support of ministers for the next fifty years. It is a
significant piece of legislation. It states specifically the amount
each person was to give. For example, those designated as
"tithable persons" were to give ten pounds of tobacco and a
bushel of corn. The same was required of all youths sixteen
years of age or older and of all Negro women. November 20,
unless it fell on Sunday, was designated as the day on which
payments were to be made. The ministers were warned to be
present. Finally, the legislators put "teeth" into the law by stating the penalty for not abiding as follows:

> And it is further ordered that if any planter or
> parishioner do neglect the bringing of the corn
> or tob'c. as aforsaid, he or they for such default
> shall forfeit double the quantity of tob'c. or corne
> to be leavied by distresses by the authority of the
> commander.[32]

Provisions for the minister were carried out in the manner
recommended above until an enactment of the Virginia Assembly in September, 1696, which allowed every established minister a yearly support of 16,000 pounds of tobacco, plus their
"lawful perquisits." [33] Exchange on tobacco was at the rate of
approximately six pence a pound which gave the clergy a salary
of 480 pounds sterling, a rather generous stipend in those days!

Tobacco was used as tender in the southern colonies because
it was the most stable medium of exchange. As noted previously,
in the New Amsterdam (New York) area, badger skins or wheat
were the most stable. Wampum fluctuated in value from day to
day, and it seemed to be the fortune of the Dutch ministers to

be paid in wampum. In Virginia and the Carolinas, however, the established ministers were paid in the most stable medium of exchange, tobacco.

Following the enactment of 1696—which awarded the clergy a yearly income of 16,000 pounds of tobacco—little change in support took place until 1758 when the Virginia Legislature passed the "Two-Penny Act." This year, 1758, saw a serious drought and a crop failure which made it virtually impossible for the people to pay the stated stipend. The "Two-Penny Act" was passed to relieve the financial burdens of the people. It held that for ten months all debts payable in tobacco could be paid either in tobacco or in money at the rate of eighteen shillings and eight pence per hundred pounds of tobacco, which reduced the price of tobacco, for the purpose of debt paying, to two pence per pound. This struck two-thirds off the ministerial salary. What did the clergymen do? They denounced the law and proceeded to bring lawsuits against the laity.

The most famous of these was the suit of the Reverend James Maury in 1763. The court declared the act of 1758 invalid, as not approved by the king. During the case, popular feeling was that the whole question was practically decided in favor of the clergy. When it looked as if the whole case was going to pass by default, the laymen took for their advocate a young man who had failed in business, but who, after reading law for a few weeks, was admitted to the bar, conditionally. His appeal won the case and established him as "the leading jury lawyer of Virginia." His name was Patrick Henry. After this defeat, the clergy attempted no further suits. The damage they suffered cannot be measured by the decreased salary. The ministers were described as having no concern for the poverty and burdens of the people, and only desirous of obtaining the last penny for themselves.[34]

It is revealed in this "Parson's Case," just as it was revealed in the incidents of enforced tithes and enforced church rates in England, that the compulsory system of church support eventually brings pastor and people into the law courts. The clergy, it is true, won some cases, but, in the final results, the losses far outweighed the material gains.

The next year (1784) Patrick Henry introduced into the House of Burgesses a proposal to tax the people for the support of the Christian religion.[35] It was voted and a committee was appointed to draft the necessary bill, but the bill itself was defeated, owing to the persistence of James Madison, who insisted upon freedom:

> Who does not see that the same authority which can establish Christianity to the exclusion of all other religions may establish, with the same ease, any particular sect of Christians in exclusion of all other sects? That the same authority which can force a citizen to contribute three pence only of his property for the support of any one establishment, may force him to conform to any other establishment, in all cases whatsoever. . . . The proposed establishment is a departure from that generous policy, which, offering an assylum to the persecuted and oppressed of every nation and religion, promised a lustre to our country and an accession to the number of its citizens. . . .[36]

Nearly two centuries passed in the settlement of Virginia before men in authority began to see clearly the principles of religious freedom which inherently call for freedom from compulsory support of organized religion.

The Carolinas. Basically, the philosophy of an established church in the Carolinas was the same as in Virginia; however, circumstances placed definite limitations on Anglicanism. Although an attempt was made to colonize the Carolina area as early as 1584, by 1591 little trace remained of the first white settlers. The territory below the 36th parallel was granted (in 1629) by Charles I to Sir Robert Heath and was named Carolina in the king's honor. There was no further attempt at colonizing until 1656, when several Virginians bought land from the Indians. In 1663, Charles II made an extensive grant to eight of his favorites, who became known as the lord's proprietors and who divided the territory into North and South Carolina.[37]

The proprietaries entered into an "Agreement" with certain "adventurers," declaring freedom of worship,[38] and although the General Assembly was given power to appoint ministers and establish maintenance, liberty was given "to any person or persons to keep and mainteyne w (what) preachers or Ministers they please." [39]

Nonetheless, in the very next year, the "Fundamental Constitutions" established the Church of England and ordered it to be supported by a grant of parliament.[40] Anglicanism had been established, but other religions were given liberty to build churches and to call ministers. In fact, the ninety-seventh article of the Constitutions is one of the most remarkable decrees of toleration on record.[41]

Legislation took a turn for the worse in 1704, when an act established the Church of England and disfranchised the nonconformists. By a small majority the assembly passed two acts which outraged a majority of the people. The first required all members of the legislature to be of the Church of England and to have received the sacrament in that church at least once in the year past. The second act was "for establishing Religious worship according to the Church of England," and entered into much detail as to erection of churches, support of ministers, glebes, parishes, and the choice of ministers, vestries, clerks, and sextons, fixing even the salaries of clerk and sexton at ten pounds and five pounds. The protests against this legislation, led the queen—two years later—to declare the laws void.[42]

In South Carolina, by an act of 1715, each person was assessed five shillings per poll; and in 1722 an act increased the stipend of country parsons from fifty to one hundred pounds and gave the parson authority to collect it by the help of the receiver-general.[43]

The Act for Settling a Ministry and Raising a Maintenance for Them in the City of New York, County of Richmond, Westchester, and Queen's County. This act, finally passed September 22, 1693, was a most significant piece of legislation. A bill of this sort was proposed on April 10, 1691, by Governor Henry Sloughter, but it was rejected. A second attempt to establish such an act in the province failed the following year. Then, in his opening address, October 24, 1692, Governor Fletcher urged attention to "the support and encouragement of an able ministry." [44] Again, the next year, March 22, 1693, Governor Fletcher spoke of this matter.[45] And, on April 10 of the same year, the governor expressed his hope that the matter of ministerial provision would be placed as the first item on the docket at the next meeting.[46]

Finally, the act was passed September 22, 1693. It came only through the strong and respected recommendations of the governor, rather than from the Assembly or the people. It provided for the levying of a tax, a stated amount for the ministers, support for the poor, and a tax collector and his compensation.[47]

This act became a strong instrument in the hands of the Church of England. It received the approval of the king in 1697. Going a step further, an Act for the Better Establishment of the Maintenance for the Ministers of the City of New York was passed June 19, 1703. It empowered the constable to confiscate a person's household goods and sell them at auction, as was done in England, if he refused to pay the assessment.[48]

Still another bill was passed (August 4, 1705) to protect the interests of the Church of England—not only in the city of New

York, but also in the County of Richmond, Westchester, and Queens County.[49] This bill imposed fines on justices and vestrymen who failed to levy the required tax. The burden placed upon non-Anglican churches by this action is illustrated by the Presbyterian Church of Jamaica, where the town vestry was fined for refusing to levy the tax.[50]

Under Governor Cornbury (June 27, 1704) an act was passed that assured Trinity Church of adequate support and helped to establish the Church of England in the City of New York.[51] Under this act, Trinity Church became a corporation and became the sole recipient of the taxes that continued to be levied on the inhabitants of New York. The power to choose the vestrymen, who in turn levied the tax, was in the hands of Anglicans only. The officials of Trinity Church had the sole disposition of all monies and had the power to set the various fees connected with religious life.

Unquestionably, this marked the high point in Anglicanism as the established church. Growing opposition, during the next few years, convinced Anglicans their establishment was threatened. A letter written in 1714, by some Anglicans to the Bishop of London, contained a detailed account of the welfare of the Church of England in and around the City of New York, stating, "we of the Communion of the established church seem strangers in the land." [52]

Opposition to the Ministry Act continued to grow, Anglican leaders began to admit in their correspondence to the Bishop of London and to the Society for Propagating the Gospel that lack of ministers of the Church of England was defeating their cause. During the year 1770, the matter of repealing the Ministry Act of 1693 was before the Assembly no less than fifteen times. At last, on April 20, 1777, the act with all its amendments was repealed.

It took another six years before a positive piece of legislation was passed, giving freedom to religious groups. It came on April 6, 1784, when a far-reaching action was taken, enabling all religious denominations in the state to appoint trustees and to provide support for their various expenses.[53]

Enforced support dominated the church life in early New England, New Netherland (New York), and some of the southern colonies. The various philosophies of compulsory support differed slightly, but all held one conviction in common: purity of religion depends on state supervision and support.

It is generally true that religious life was at a low ebb during this period of enforced support. One cannot be sure whether compulsory support creates religious indifference or whether religious indifference makes compulsory support necessary. The two seem to go together. It is quite certain, however, that enforced support has a tendency to alienate the public from the church. Under systems of compulsion the clergy frequently have found it necessary to bring their people to court. The "Parson's Case" was probably the most notable instance in which the clergy sacrificed good will and service for financial gain.

When a church must seek support by compulsion and by taxing nonbelievers, there is something inherently wrong. Benjamin Franklin spoke some words of wisdom on this subject, saying:

> When a religion is good, I conceive it will support itself; and when it does not support itself, and God does not take care to support it, so that its professors are obliged to call for help of the civil power, 'tis a sign, I apprehend, of its being a bad one.[54]

VIII

Methods
of Support

The previous chapters outlined the philosophies of church support which motivated the financial maneuvers of the church in early America. Now, specific methods for raising money for the support of the ministers in these early days must be considered. The growth and development of these various methods can be grouped in the following order: (1) glebes, (2) pew revenues, (3) collections and offerings, (4) subscription lists, and (5) lotteries.

Glebes

A glebe is the land or farm belonging to—or yielding revenue to—a church or ecclesiastical benefice. In England and on the Continent, before and after the Reformation, this was a common source of support for the clergy. The idea was brought to America by the first settlers, and in almost every colony the church made use of the glebe.

A case in point is the first minister sent to New Netherland, Jonas Michaelius,[1] who spoke of the glebe that had been awarded to him—some acres of land. It was not profitable since there were "no horses, cows, or laborers to be obtained here for money."[2]

In the colonies where Anglicanism had been established, a

glebe was granted as a part of the minister's support; and in Virginia, each parish of the Established Church of England was granted—by the government—a glebe purchased with public funds.

Almost from the outset, the church at Jamaica provided a few acres for the minister, as well as a cash salary and parsonage. Zechariah Walker, a licentiate, the first minister to serve the church, had his salary fixed on February 14, 1663, but on March 2, 1663, the use of the house and lot was added by action of the town.[3]

Examples of glebes throughout New Hampshire, Connecticut, and Massachusetts give evidence that a farm or parsonage lot was included as part of the minister's support. Of course, the glebe varied from place to place.

Ecumenicity was demonstrated in Cornish, New Hampshire, when in 1763, after laying out two hundred acres of land for the Church of England, two hundred acres for the Society for the Propagation of the Gospel, and two hundred acres for the first settled minister, as the town was required to do, the citizens also voted at least one hundred fifty acres of good land set apart toward supporting a dissenting minister.[4]

At first, the minister lived on the glebe and worked the land in the same manner his neighbors worked their farms. There was some objection to the minister's spending time farming, just as there were objections to his teaching, "marchandizing," or practicing medicine. One deacon indicated both the drawback and the advantage of the farmer-preacher: "Wa'll, our minister gives so much attention to his farm and orchard that we get pretty poor sermons, but he is mighty movin' in prayer in canter-piller and cankerworm time."[5] On the negative side, the glebe divided a minister's time; but, on the positive side, it helped him to understand better the trials of his people.

After a time, the ministers of churches rented out the glebe or farm and used the cash income for expenses. The next step was, of course, to sell the farm.

The amount of actual support derived from the glebes varied with each parish. Timothy Walker, an early New England minister, made entries in his diary,[6] revealing his annual salary as one hundred twenty pounds, plus a glebe—the "encouragement" as it was called—giving him an adequate supply of pork, beef, vegetables, and cider.

A full appreciation of the value of the glebe can be had only by understanding the devastating effects of inflation in those days. Since ministers were always victims of the fluctuating value of currency, the glebe became a hedge against inflation.

Between 1776 and 1780, with the heavy issue of paper money by state and local banks, inflation made financial matters difficult for the minister. The North Hampton Church voted their minister, David McClure, $500 in addition to his salary for the year 1778; and the next year they again voted him 1,000 extra dollars. The year after that, it was increased forty to one! Yet, his salary bought little.[7] Consequently, the man who had a tie to the land was saved from some of the hardships inflicted by inflation.

The glebe or "homestead" method of supporting the ministry in the Methodist Church was the exception rather than the rule. Francis Asbury noted in his *Journal* that local preachers were free to keep plantations and slaves, but the demands of the itineracy did not allow this of traveling preachers.[8]

With few exceptions, the glebe was a popular method by which the colonial churches and the churches on the American frontier helped to support their ministers. Many rural churches practice the glebe method to the present day, called by a different term, however—"a church farm," or "pastor's homestead."

Pew Revenues

It is difficult to detect any particular pattern which American churches followed in using pews as a source of income. A number of factors determined the method of selling, renting, or assessing pews. A meetinghouse built with town-tax or colony-tax money could begin at once to sell or to rent the pews. On the other hand, a church without a building may have had to build the meetinghouse first and then allow individuals to build their own personal pews. In another situation, the town built the meetinghouse, and the pews were assigned by a committee; then the pewholders were assessed. In still a different situation, the pews were sold to raise money to build the meetinghouse and the town tax took care of the minister's salary.

It is almost impossible to find a chronological order in the development of the pew revenue idea. However, the practice expressed itself in the following ways: privately built pews, pews assigned by a committee, pews sold, pews rented, pews assessed, and the return to free pews.

Pews Privately Built. Many of the early meetinghouses were built without seats of any kind. People knelt on the floor to pray, stood to sing, and stood to listen to the sermon. In some cases, a seat first appeared for the minister's family. In other cases, an individual made application for the privilege of building a pew for his family. Many times, plain benches preceded the individually built pews. For example, there were no pews in the second meetinghouse in Bridgeport, Connecticut, in 1717. Gradually, families were permitted to erect their own. A Mr. Cooke led the way by petitioning the Society: "Your petitioner requests your favour so far as to grant me the liberty of making a pew for my wife and children at my own charge in the new meetinghouse, on the women's side of the pulpit." [9]

In the new meetinghouse in Stonington, Connecticut, completed January 15, 1673, there were no pews, except for the deacons, magistrates, and minister's family. There were, however, benches for the rest of the people.[10] The next year, the town voted to have the floor of the house and of the gallery assigned to the inhabitants, where they might build their own pews.

The fourth meetinghouse in Hampton, New Hampshire, had only one pew and that was for the minister's family. Later, other pews were built by individuals.[11] A slight variation is seen in the action of the Goffstown Congregational Church, New Hampshire, in that as late as 1769 the "pew ground" (upon which each might construct his own pew) was sold at auction.[12]

As one might expect, a few problems arose over the ownership of the pews built by individuals. It was the issue of pew ownership that called forth a detailed action by the congregation of Old South Church, Boston, October 26, 1685. The seventh paragraph covering the action gave a man liberty to turn his pew over to his children, but denied him the right to sell it or to turn it over to one outside the family without the consent of the "overseers." If the pew owner desired to leave the church, he was to be reimbursed, then the church could resell the pew. In case two families were interested in one seat, the overseers were empowered to settle the controversy. If the parties were not satisfied with the decision, the matter was placed before the civil authority.[13]

Pew or "Pew Ground" Assigned. In the colonial period, the place in which one worshiped within the church was an important consideration. In 1700—when only the minister's family had a pew in the Hampton Church—even the crude seats were assigned to the people by a committee. It is interesting—and perhaps significant—to note that one's wealth or financial contribution was not always the factor which decided his location. In the church at Stamford, on July 4, 1710, the congregation decided for a more orderly seating in the meetinghouse, ". . . and suitable respect given unto civil authority, age, and military commission office, commissioned by the court." [14] Even before pews were built in the Stonington Church, a committee assigned the people to the benches, "according to their notions of propriety." [15] After seats became more uniform in the Bridgeport Church, a committee was appointed to seat the members by dignity, age, and estate.

Sale of Pews. Church histories do not always make clear whether pews were sold or rented. Therefore, regardless of the terms "sell" or "rent," this study considers a pew *sold* only if it became the property of the buyer. If a man "bought" a pew for one year, it is considered a rented pew.

When pews began to be sold at auction, "dignity," "age," or "civil authority" ceased to be guiding factors in seating the people. The highest bidders owned and occupied the choice seats. And, if the people had reacted then as they do today, the rich would have had the back seats and the poor would have had to sit in front. In that day, however, the choice seats were near the front! From an entry in the minutes of the Old South Church, it appears that all pews had a set price of ten pounds, until April 21, 1721, when that price was annulled, and thereafter the prices varied.

When the congregation of Old South Church decided to build a new building in 1728, the committee on pews was faced with the rights of pew owners in the old building. It made the following decisions [16]: (1) the pews in the new church, as in the old, became the personal property of the owners; (2) eleven articles were drawn to govern pew holders.

In the first place, it was considered good order for each person to have an assigned seat. Second, each person was expected to support the church in proportion "to the privilege" he enjoyed, which probably meant in proportion to the value of his particular pew. Third, a man's pew was his personal property; he could will it to his heirs or sell it. If he did not comply with the regulations of the church, he might have had to surrender it by default, but even in this case the church would have paid him the original cost of the pew. Also, he had to have the approval of the church before he sold his pew. A fourth significant point is the emphasis placed on the pew as revenue producing. To wit: if the children were unable to pay the assessments made against their pew, others would be assigned to sit with them. And one article indicated the minimum annual contribution expected from the various pew holders. The last article guarded against one member—or a few members—gaining a monopoly. If a man had a pew and fell heir to another, the committee was authorized to dispose of one of the pews and pay the man the established price.

Considerable dissension was caused by the many pew transactions. The pastor of Old South Church, Joseph Sewall, gives evidence in his diary of a few stormy sessions over the matter of pew rents:

> We had a Church-Meeting to determine the way
> in which the Subscribers are to Choose their Pews.
> O Lord govern this matter in mercy; keep us in
> Peace. Mr. Prince and I had prayed together with
> an especial regard to this Affair; And this day I
> again commended it to God.[17]

After all had chosen their pews, the pastor wrote, "O Lord, I thank thee for the peace we enjoy."

Often, churches first sold their pews, then later wished to recall them and rent them on a yearly basis. Accordingly, on December 20, 1838, the Session of the Presbyterian Church of Franklin, Ohio, took up the matter of raising support for the coming year and "agreed to make an effort to have the seats sold (rented) for the support of the Gospel annually, if the owners wud (*sic*) give them up." [18]

Since pew rents largely made up the minister's salary, they have not remained steady throughout the years. The Pine Street Presbyterian Church, Philadelphia, paid for the church building by a lottery and raised the minister's salary by renting pews. The pews were selected by the congregation, February 23, 1768, immediately after the church was built. One hundred pews were taken the first day.[19] Five years later, that congregation was able to increase the minister's salary only after the pew rents were advanced. Later, decreasing pew rents made it necessary for the pastor, Dr. Allen, to relinquish $750 from his salary. When pew rents were not equal to the necessary expenses, other means were devised by which to raise money. Therefore, in 1864, to supplement the pew rents in Carlisle, Pennsylvania, a $200 subscription was raised. The next year, the pew rents were increased, again, to eliminate the subscriptions.[20]

The practice of renting pews in Methodist churches was confined to the larger towns where Episcopal, Congregational, and Presbyterian influence was strong. The Methodists resolved "that the manner of building houses of religious worship with pews is contrary to the rules of our economy, and inconsistent with the interests of our societies." These sentiments became a part of the Methodist Discipline in 1820 when it was stated, "Let all our chapels be built plain and decent and with free seats." [21]

This, however, did not put a stop to the practice of renting pews in the Methodist Church, rather the practice had extended more and more through the eastern and northern conferences, causing the people to plead "the necessity of the case for a departure in this respect from the primitive usage of Methodism." [22]

Return to "Free" Seats. For at least one hundred fifty years, the pew-rent system of church support was under criticism.

Critics have attacked the system in a variety of ways. One man made light of the system in a lengthy poem, from which the following is taken:

"Who'll buy this pew?" the salesman cries:
"Location good—a pleasant size.
Two hundred-fifty-three—go on—
Three fifty—four—five—going—gone.
Who'll have the next? Best in the church—
Bid up—don't leave us in the lurch.
'Tis gone. The next! They must be sold.
Come, gentlemen, don't mind your gold;
Money enough, when you are gone,
For sons-in-law to revel on.
Three hundred bid? Well done, I say;
We'll make a splendid sale to-day,
It can't be beat—the stock is good—
First rate—I see I'm understood.
Bid up! Now show that you're alive;
Three fifty—four—four fifty—five—
Five hundred dollars for this pew—
Going at five—a bargain, too—
'Tis gone. It is yours, Mr. Great;
I do you, sir, congratulate.

"All now are sold, except two more—
Those in the corner, near the door;
But since they're kept for charity,
I've been advised to let them be.
For your attendance thanks are due;
My thanks I give, kind sirs, to you."

Thus, by this plan (the very best),
The principal and interest
Of money lent can be repaid;
It yields the church substantial aid.
You see, the man who owns the pew,
If he should choose, can sell it too.
If things succeed, there is a chance
The pew in value will advance.

There is our neighbor, Mr. K.,
Who sold his pew the other day;
Four hundred dollars he had paid—
He sold the pew for six, and made
A handsome profit by the trade.
The furniture he sold by lot,
And more than what it cost he got.
I do not say that there are any
Who join the church to make a penny;
But in a case like this, you see,
A pew is not bad property.[23]

About 1870, some churches began discontinuing the pew-rent system and in its place adopted either a freewill offering or a pledge-and-envelope system. In 1872, for example, the German Presbyterian Church, Germantown, Pennsylvania, radically changed the financial system by abandoning the pew-rent system and instituting a method by which each individual decided for himself what he would pay. Each family was assigned a pew, but no price was charged. Also, a pew carried the name of a particular family which occupied it faithfully from the pew-rent system to the pledge-and-envelope system.

In the first year of Germantown's new experiment some $4,600 was subscribed and paid, instead of $2,000 which had been the largest sum ever paid for pew rents. The next year, it was $5,600 and continued between $5,500 and $6,000 for years following.[24] More important, it removed the price tag from the privilege of having a pew, yet it retained the value of the family pew, which was the ground on which many stood in their reluctance to give up the pew-rent system.

Sometime in the 1880's, the sexton of "the most fashionable church of the Protestant Episcopal Communion on Manhattan Island" advised a stranger, a poorly dressed woman, to go to one of the chapels maintained by the church instead of trying to worship in the main edifice. The story got into the newspapers, and one editor wrote the following in *The Dana Sun:*

> You can pray at the Joss House in Mott Street,
>   With never a cent to pay;
> But you can't do that at St. Thomas,
>   For it isn't built up that way.[25]

Writing in *The Spectator,* 1896, one commentator indicated the growing attitude of many people against the pew-rented church in the following description:

> ... a building divided into wooden pews, after the
> manner of a cattle market, with the entrance to
> each pen secured against intruders by lock and key,
> and the interior adorned by various arrangements
> of cushion and hassock.[26]

As late as 1914, *The Literary Digest* carried an article, entitled, "Is Christ in the Rented Pew?" The author contended the church which rents its pews is a church which encourages class consciousness. Such a church, he claimed, is "the private leasehold of the pew-renters." In the same way, he attacked the system for having free seats for the poor. This, he said, makes the poor "the relics of a feudal system that has been extinct everywhere except in the Church for some four hundred years." [27]

Trinity Church, New York, adopted the policy of free pews immediately after World War I—"... as an expression of thanksgiving to Almighty God for the victory." [28] If this was done as an expression of gratitude, the act must have been considered the right thing to do in the sight of God!

About this time, the *New York Evening Post* published the statements of two leading New York clergymen who spoke out against the rented pew.[29] The first, Dr. Henry Sloane Coffin, compared the church to a neighborhood school rather than an exclusive club. Christians are more eager for the religiously indifferent and unenlightened to be reached than in their own preferential treatment; hence, they ought to prefer to stand, if necessary, that the casual attendant may be seated where he will hear most satisfactorily. The second clergyman, Dr. Ernest M. Stires, then of St. Thomas' Episcopal Church, expressed his convictions briefly and clearly by saying: "If the renting of pews prevents Christian hospitality in any church, then that church should quickly change its method."

As the trend to free seats continued, a few clergymen tried to defend rented pews. Their defense was weak. Once the system was examined seriously in the light of the evangelical mission of the church, pew revenue was replaced by other methods.

In summarizing the case against pew revenues, it can be said, in the first instance, that it failed to provide adequate support for the church. Churches frequently had difficulty in collecting pew rents. In many churches a pew collector had to be employed. Various pressures had to be brought to bear upon the negligent. In some cases, the right of the pew was taken from the individual if he failed to pay. Some paid, but others merely left the church. Fines were assessed against delinquent renters, but this brought only slight results. The Donegal Presbytery at one time went so far as to pass a law providing that any person in arrears on his pledge or rent was to be excluded, with his entire family, from the Lord's Supper, and was to be refused baptism for his children.[30] Such action comes dangerously close to putting a price on the sacraments, which is a form of simony.

Second, the system failed to carry out the principle of proportionate giving. It is true that the seats, often, were sold or rented at auction and at different prices, but the prices undoubtedly failed to be in proportion to the financial ability of the individuals. The poor widow would have been unable to attend unless she should take a "free" seat, reserved for the poor. There was no conception of her being the "greatest giver," since in the pew-rent system, he who gave the most in pounds or dollars was awarded the choice seat.

In the third place, the rented pew created a class consciousness. The better seats rented for a higher price; therefore, the better seats, naturally, attracted the people with more wealth. Consequently, the poor would be congregated in one section and the rich in another.

A fourth objection to the system is its violation of the voluntary principle. It is true that a man was free either to buy or not to buy. But, if he wished to attend, the price of his sitting was assigned. Any assessment such as this detracts from the voluntary spirit.

Finally, the pew-rent system was not compatible with an evangelical church. It discouraged visitors and new people from attending the services. Ideally, a man should not be expected to support the church until he has consecrated himself to it. Contrary to that ideal, in the pew-revenue system, one was expected to buy or rent a pew *before* he would be allowed to hear the Word.

Collections and Offerings

When Sunday offerings or collections were introduced in American churches, they were designated for specific objects and were taken on special occasions. For example, offerings for the poor were taken at the time of Holy Communion, and were called "table money." In some churches, an annual "Charity Sermon" was delivered, and an offering was taken for the poor. In the Brick Presbyterian Church, New York, these funds were given to the deacons who attended, personally, to the distribution of the money.[31]

Thanksgiving Day was another popular occasion for receiving a collection, especially among Congregational Churches. The purpose of these offerings varied and was left to the decision of the officials. It was never used for routine expenses; instead, these gifts financed special causes. The minister's salary and the regular expenses of the church were met by pew rents or sales, subscriptions, and assessments collected apart from services of worship.

Of course, there were exceptions. Even prior to 1800, some churches took a collection at every service for the "support of the gospel," and these funds, along with pew rents, provided for salaries and regular expenses.

Thus, as one would expect, the benevolence—or missionary program—of the churches was supported, almost entirely, by special offerings. The Presbyterian Synod appealed to the churches, in 1719, to take a yearly collection "for the carrying on of the said noble and pious design of planting and spreading the everlasting Gospel in these Provinces." [32]

A growing number of groups—some religious and some secular—began to request permission to put on a program in the churches and receive a special offering. By the end of the first quarter of the nineteenth century, some city churches found it necessary to regulate the number of offerings that could be taken in the course of a year. A typical example was the Brick Presbyterian Church in New York City where—between 1818 and 1838—no less than 43 societies received special offerings. The Session of Brick Church decided to exclude agents of benevolent groups and ordered all appeals to be made by the pastor; also, a charge of $25 was made for the use of the church by outside groups. [33]

As pew-rent systems were discontinued and as benevolence of a church was given a more systematic place in the financial program of the churches, offerings and collections became one of the primary methods of support. Nevertheless, even to the present day, some churches depend upon special offerings in addition to the regular offering.

The development of the collection in American Methodism—in some respects—was similar to the other churches; however, because of the unique approach of Methodism to financial matters, her changing attitudes toward collections deserve an additional comment. At first there was some question about a weekly collection. At a meeting of Methodist preachers (December 23, 1772) the matter was considered; and it was asked, "Shall we make collections weekly to pay the preachers' board and expenses?" The record merely states, "This was not agreed to." [34]

There were, however, frequent collections to meet various other needs. In 1775, the Conference passed a resolution to raise a yearly collection for general purposes.[35] Later the same year, it was voted that both the expense of Thomas Rankin, general assistant, and the expenses of the preachers from Conference to their circuits were to be paid out of the yearly collection.[36] And, in 1781, it was agreed that every assistant was to inform all the societies of the sum that was to be paid for the preachers' quarterage, exclusive of traveling expenses, and to urge them to give according to their several abilities.[37] Faced with the problem of raising funds for the support of preachers' wives, the group voted (in 1783) to "make a small collection in all the circuits." [38]

Several significant steps were taken at the "Christmas Conference" of 1784, when a full statement of collections was made. In the first place, quarterly collections were urged, as well as yearly collections. Second, it was recommended that collections be taken for specific projects—building churches, relief to the poor, and supporting the college. Third, five "public" collections were specified, plus four quarterly collections for the preachers, and one yearly collection for "contingencies" of the Conference. Also, a collection was to be made at every annual conference and General Conference for the support of the ministry.

A major change occurred in 1808, as the General Conference

gave the annual conference the liberty to adopt such plans as necessary to raise the required funds.[39] Further liberty was granted to the conferences four years later, when the General Conference granted them the right to decide the means by which the salaries of preachers were to be raised.[40] And in 1832, the General Conference ordered weekly collections to be taken in all societies "where it is practicable." [41] It took sixty years (the preachers first discussed weekly collections in 1772) to move into a full emphasis on weekly offerings.

Another significant development in the matter of collections took place in 1834. A controversy had arisen over the collections ordered by the General Conference for specific purposes. It seems that some boards of trustees claimed the right, by virtue of their corporate powers, to take possession of all monies collected in the churches for specific objects—or in the ordinary way—and appropriate them as they wished. In opposition to this claim, it was pleaded that monies raised for any specific purpose must be appropriated as designated.

A leading lawyer of the day ruled that money given into the Methodist Church was not given to the corporation, but rather to the annual conference, insisting, "The corporation are trustees only for the congregations who meet in their churches. The money has been given for the use of all the congregations under the jurisdiction of the conference." [42] Even the clergy had no jurisdiction of the monies collected. This lawyer, by the name of Jay, a son of Governor Jay, further stated that the trustees could not prohibit rightfully the collections directed by the Book of Discipline from being made in their churches.[43]

A rather uniform pattern can be seen in the development of offerings and collections. At first, they were received only a few times during the year and were designated for special projects. In time, the projects increased in number, partly through an expanding program within the denomination and partly through the advantage taken by outside organizations to present a program at a church service and receive an offering. Hence, some churches were compelled to regulate the special offerings. Early in the nineteenth century, nearly all churches urged special collections for missions. Again, at this point, some churches found it necessary to impose regulations, since denominational boards increased the number of collections by sending agents into the congregations to raise offerings.

The multiple offerings and collections in American churches, probably, did more than anything else to show the need of business methods and a unified approach in the seeking of funds. People became weary of frequent appeals, business-minded men objected to the unplanned approach. As a result, fertile ground was at hand for the seeds of the unified budget.

Subscription Lists

Subscriptions or subscription lists are a form of pledge in money—or in kind—toward some project of the church. Generally, in the past, they were for a new church building, extensive repairs, or the minister's salary. Occasionally, subscription lists were circulated for a variety of less important needs. This method was employed as a natural successor to the taxation method. Under the taxation method, the amount was assigned to the individual according to his estate, but in the subscription procedure, the individual decided the amount he would give. In both cases, however, one's estate was a guiding factor, since legal compulsion set the individual's share under taxation, but social pressure determined the amount a man put on the subscription list. Some committees went to the extreme of indicating on the subscription list the general amount each individual was to give.

With few exceptions, the subscription list followed a simple pattern in which an individual, or a committee, circulated a paper on which members and friends stated the amount they intended to give. One secret of success in circulating the subscription paper was to have the largest givers subscribe first. This would encourage others to keep their pledges high. Another factor was the practice of giving the highest subscriber to a new church building first choice in the selection of pews.

An interesting variation in the pattern of circulating a subscription list for a new church building occurred in New Netherland in 1642. At the suggestion of Captain DeVries, the director of the Colony, a Mr. Kieft took up the idea of a new meetinghouse; it was approved by the wardens, but money was lacking. Not to be stymied, advantage was taken of the wedding of Domine Borgardus' daughter. The wine was plentiful, the guests became somewhat hilarious, and DeVries subscribed a hundred guilders toward a new church! He circulated a subscription list, asking the guests to do the same. With light heads and merry hearts, they subscribed, handsomely! Later, in more sober moments, many persons wished to alter their subscriptions, but they were held to them by the town authority.[44]

To the Methodists, the subscription paper was quite acceptable as a method of raising money for new chapels and churches. Soon after 1770, the John Street Society set the precedent for Methodists in taking subscriptions in America by having 129 people sign either their names or their initials, along with the amount of their pledge.[45]

The General Conference, in 1808, further authorized subscriptions to be taken among the more wealthy societies to help pay the debt on the house of worship in Boston.[46] Asbury himself set forward a subscription list for building a house of worship in Middlebury.[47]

Methodism on the frontier allowed, and encouraged, subscription lists for missions,[48] accepting pledges of lumber, nails, or time of man and time of work animals. In time, subscription lists were circulated to raise support for the minister.

However, the Baptists did not approve of the subscription list for the minister's support. The story is told of one deacon, moved to action by his minister's poverty, who circulated a subscription list only to be met with so much opposition that he returned to the pastor and reported he "was sorry that he had undertaken it." [49] After a subscription list had been used in a Missouri congregation for the Baptist Board of Foreign Missions, a majority of the members actually rose up and demanded the subscription papers be brought forward and burned.[50]

Churches—other than Baptists and Methodists—generally used the subscription list to support ministers. There was no limit to the variety of items appearing on these lists. Firewood was always important. Occasionally, whisky was listed. For instance, a list for the salary of Joshua L. Wilson, First Presbyterian Church of Cincinnati, for the year 1807, listed 222 gallons of whisky! In addition, the 84 subscribers pledged 40 bushels of wheat, 100 pounds of beef, 21 yards of linen, 1,420 pounds of pork, 700 pounds of flour, and money amounting to 13 pounds and 8 shillings.[51]

The South Elkhorn Baptist Congregation raised a subscription for their pastor in 1798. The items were listed in ten columns with the following headings: "Cash, Salt, Corn 1s Barr, Wheat 1s Bu, park 1b, flower 1b, beaf 1b, Sugar 1b, Tallow 1b, and Whisky Galln." All the columns had amounts indicated or checked, except the column headed "Tallow 1b." A total of 36 gallons of whisky was promised the preacher.[52] It is not surprising that the most frequent cause for discipline of ministers in early America was overindulgence in strong drink!

How successful were subscription lists? Apparently, pledges toward new buildings were paid, eventually. The Presbyterian Church of Dayton attempted to guard against unpaid pledges with the stipulation that subscriptions were payable "when the walls of the meetinghouse are raised one store high." [53] The implication seems to be: pledges had to be paid before the building would proceed further.

Subscription lists toward the pastor's salary, undoubtedly, gave the congregation and the pastor an idea of how much support could be expected. In fact, Presbyterian pastors frequently refused calls to churches until the subscription list had been circulated. Such a case was the First Presbyterian Church, Phelps, New York, where negotiations with a candidate were discontinued when the subscriptions were not adequate.[54]

The subscription method was a forerunner of the pledge system which has come into wide use in the twentieth century. Actually, the subscription list is still circulated today, even with the questionable procedure of "baiting" the list with the highest giver's name and pledge at the top of the list.

Lotteries

The New International Encyclopedia defines the lottery as "a game of chance wherein a large number of persons unite to create a fund out of which prizes, greatly exceeding in value any individual contribution, are assigned by lot to a small number of participants." [55] This definition does not cover all forms of lotteries, but it does define the lotteries used by churches in early America.[56]

The lottery has been traced back to the days of ancient Rome, where it was used by Augustus Caesar as a method of entertainment at dinner parties. The earliest clear record of what might be called a commercial lottery appears in 1420 in the town records of L'Ecluse, then part of the realm of the dukes of Burgundy; it was used to raise money for strengthening the town's fortifications.[57]

Queen Elizabeth I sponsored the first English lottery in 1569, to be used "towards the reparation of the avens and strength of the Realme and towards such other publique goode works." [58] As an inducement for all to come and buy, it was announced that, for seven days, any ticket buyer would be safe from arrest for anything except major crimes. Superstition—which is a part of all gambling—was evident, in that people did not use their real names, believing it would bring bad luck to use a real name. Frequently, they signed up under a "device," or "posie," examples of which follow:

> Wee put in one lott, poor maydens we be ten
> Wee pray God send us a good lott, that all wee
>   may say Amen.

> God send good lott for my children and me
> Which have had twenty by one wife truly.

> From Hastings we come, God send good speed.
> Never a poor fisher town in England of ye great
>   lott
> hath more need.[59]

America first came under the influence of the lottery when King James allowed the Virginia Company of London, 1612, "to set forth, erect, and publish one or more lottery or lotteries, to have continuance for the space of one whole year next after the opening of the same." [60] London churches shared in this adventure.[61]

The earliest public announcement for an American lottery appeared in Andrew Bradford's *American Weekly Mercury,* Philadelphia, February 23, 1720.[62] For the next hundred years, churches and respected citizens participated in lotteries. George Washington and Benjamin Franklin were among those who participated in lotteries of their day. Ministers, also, entered into schemes. An extract from the diary of the Reverend Samuel Seabury, father of Bishop Seabury, indicates his faith that God had a hand in his success in a lottery in which he won "500 pounds sterling." [63]

To the best of this writer's knowledge, the first lottery for a church was held by the Trenton Presbyterian Church, 1749. It was held for the purpose of "finishing the church at Trenton" and was drawn in Pennsylvania, because lotteries were prohibited by the New Jersey Legislature in 1748. Later, in 1754, the minister of the Trenton Presbyterian Church, the Rev. Mr. Cowell, advertised tickets for sale for a lottery being conducted in Connecticut for the benefit of the College of New Jersey. [64]

A license was obtained from Governor Hamilton, in 1760, authorizing the Carlisle Presbyterian Church (Pennsylvania) to raise money by a lottery "to enable them to build a decent house for the worship of God." A few years later, the Legislature found it necessary to pass an act compelling "the managers to settle" and the "adventurers to pay." [65]

The Old Pine Street Presbyterian Church, Philadelphia, used a lottery to complete its church building; it yielded 2,500 pounds. [66] The officers of the first Methodist meetinghouse in New York, Wesley Chapel, bought a lottery ticket on March 1, 1790, in the hope that their winnings might help to build the church, [67] but subsequent records fail to indicate any winnings. This conclusion is based on an entry appearing in the early records of the New York Society: "1790, March 1. Cash paid for a ticket in the lottery £2.00. [67] There is no record on the results. Had the ticket won, the prize probably would have been entered in the book. It is probably more correct to assume the society lost money on the lottery.

Lotteries of those early days had one thing in common with the typical money-raising church dinner: there was a tremendous outlay for every dollar cleared. An example is provided by the records of the Second Presbyterian Church, Baltimore, where it took $20,450 in prizes to raise $1,411! High "overhead" indeed! The advertisement of this lottery appeared in the *American Advertiser,* March 11, 1805:

SECOND PRESBYTERIAN CHURCH LOTTERY
Authorized by the General Assembly of the State
of Maryland and the corporation of
the City of Baltimore.

Scheme

1	prize of	$5,000
1	prize of	2,000
1	prize of	1,000
3	prizes, $500 each	1,500
8	prizes, $200 each	1,600
20	prizes, $100 each	2,000
40	prizes, $50 each	2,000
200	prizes, $10 each	2,000
3,350	prizes, $1 each	3,350

The notice, also, indicated the purpose for which the money was to be used, a new church building. Incidentally, the *Telegram and Daily Advertiser,* May 21, 1805, announced the first drawing took place in a Mr. Meyer's tavern.[68]

The appeal made to the public by the First Presbyterian Church of Baltimore contains a few significant points. On July 7, 1761, the following advertisement appeared in the *Maryland Gazette:*

> *Religion,* the crowning Excellence of intelligent Nature, claims the Approbation and close Attention of every respectable Being who expects future Bliss. We are bound from Principles of Gratitude and Interest to promote the Honour and Worship of the Supreme Mind, as necessary to our own Prosperity, the God of Society, and the future Happiness of Man. Sustained by these interesting Motives, we of the Presbyterian

Persuasion in this Town desire not from Party
Views, but from real Principle, to purchase a Lot
of Ground to erect a decent Church for Divine
Service, in which we may worship GOD according
to our Consciences. Upon Enquiry we find ourselves as yet insufficient to raise such a sum as is
necessary to accomplish such an important design,
beg leave therefore to sollicit the Generosity of
our Fellow Christians to assist and encourage us
in compleating a small lottery at a time when
the Benevolence of our Countrymen is so well
tried in this Way. We hope our Claim to the
public Attention is equal to any that has solicited
their Notice and humbly expect that we shall
meet with general Encouragement.[69]

It is almost unbelievable that a group of Christians should
have to "try" the benevolent spirit of their neighbors, in order
that they (the Christians) might "promote the Honour and
Worship of the Supreme Mind," as necessary to their "own
Prosperity. . . ."

Again, people were asked to buy tickets amounting to
$20,000 to raise $3,000. Two attempts were made in this lottery, but both failed. Ten years later, another attempt was made
to initiate a new lottery, but it did not meet with success. Some
of the people did not pay their tickets in full; and, as late as
1775, long after the drawing had been made, some still had not
paid for their tickets.

One church that did succeed in a lottery was St. Paul's Protestant Episcopal Church, Baltimore, where $33,433 was raised
for a new church building in 1780.[70]

When lotteries were accepted as legitimate and honorable
ways to raise money for public projects, it was only natural that
churches made use of the system. However, when public senti-
ment and legislative action began to oppose lotteries, one would

think—or at least hope—the church would lead in the crusade to eradicate the evil. Such was not the case! Instead, when the New Jersey Legislature outlawed lotteries, the church went into other states to raise money by this means.

The conscience of the church was gradually awakened to the evils of the lottery. This probably came about with the development of lotteries for private gain. Lottery schemes for public benefits served to quiet the conscience of the scrupulous, but when they began to enrich private concerns, the church was able to see the evils more clearly. Sentiments in the church turned against lotteries as such, but the church has continued to sponsor variations of the lottery to the present day. These variations and the moral and ethical implications are discussed in the following chapter.

part **THREE**

MONEY AND THE CHURCH
IN CONTEMPORARY AMERICA

IX.   Lottery and Merchandising
      Variations of the lottery
      Bingo
      Merchandising schemes
      Church farm and Lord's Acre
      Business enterprises
      Activity and faith

X.   Every Member Canvass
      Budgets
      Education and promotion
      Pledges
      Envelopes
      Youth participation
      Secondary accomplishments
      Professional fund raisers

XI.   Motives for Giving
      Oblation and fear
      Legal compulsion
      Personal glorification
      Personal profit
      Self-interest
      Missionary
      Love

XII.   Guiding Principles
      Stewardship
      Proportionate giving
      First fruits

XIII.   The Discipline of Tithing
      A rise in interest
      Tithing defined
      Five witnesses for tithing

XIV.   The Ministry of Christian Giving
      The gospel imperative
      The meaning of money
      Money is you
      Evangelists all

IX

Lottery
and Merchandising

The churches in contemporary America—since the turn of the century—have been supported by chance, by exchange, and by gift. The more significant activities and methods can be discussed under these headings: (1) variations of the lottery, (2) bingo, (3) merchandising schemes, (4) church farm and Lord's Acre, (5) business enterprises, and (6) activities and faith.

Variations of the Lottery

The idea of the lottery has continued to the present day under the guise of raffles and other games of chance, bearing a variety of names. For example, the quilt became almost symbolic as the church-raffle prize. Frequently, the ladies of a church would work all year making quilts to be sold at the annual bazaar. Chances were sold on each quilt, and a drawing took place.

Prizes have not been confined to quilts. Early in the present century, some rural congregations in Georgia conducted a raffle which involved a bit of skill in horseback riding. A live goose with a greased neck and head was tied by its legs to a high branch of a tree. Each participant would mount his horse and at a fast pace ride under the branch within reach of the goose, reaching out and trying to pull the head off the goose. The man accomplishing the feat won the fowl. The fee for entering in such a sport was fifty cents.

The ladies of a Methodist Church in New Jersey selected a rather unusual prize for their raffle—a bronze plaque of the Lord's Supper. Chances were sold at ten cents, to the crowds attending the neighborhood theaters.

Another variation of the ordinary raffle—more common in the South—is the "Cake Walk." In this scheme, a number of cakes are donated for a church party. Just before refreshments are served, the "Cake Walk" is held. Chances on each cake are sold for amounts ranging from five cents to fifty cents. The cakes are placed on a table, one at a time, and, as music is played, those holding chances walk in a circle around the cake on the table. When the music stops, the cake goes to the person standing nearest the cake.

A Methodist Church in Massachusetts held a "nickel sale," in which a number of 25-cent items were donated for the "sale." A time clock was set to mark the end of each sale; then, the people in turn around the circle rapidly bid a nickel at a time on the item. The bidding continued in this manner until the time clock stopped, and the person making the last bid bought the item. However, all the other bidders also paid the total of their bids prior to the signal of the time clock.

In recent years, some churches have made the raffle method extremely popular by offering new automobiles as prizes. Roman Catholic churches especially have capitalized on this variation.

Bingo

Of all the variations of the lottery, no other has attained the popularity of bingo. In this game, any number of players purchase boards bearing twenty-five squares differently numbered or lettered. As numbers are drawn from a box, by the gamemaster, they are called out, then players place beans or corn on the corresponding letters on their boards. A player wins if he is the first to fill five squares in a straight line and cries "bingo" or "beano."

Bingo grew out of the "corn game"—a form of rural recreation—early in the century. Churches got involved in the corn game in the 1920's when religious organizations began to hire professional carnival men to run bazaars. As the game became more and more popular, religious leaders began to examine its ethical implications. There was disagreement as to the ethics of the practice in both Protestant and Roman Catholic churches. Likewise, state legislators varied in their views. Michigan's governor, Frank D. Fitzgerald, vetoed a bill legalizing bingo in 1935. Later, he decided to allow charity games, but to stamp out commercial ones. He reversed his stand shortly after, however, and arrested a Mrs. Girodat who had sponsored a game for the Catholic Daughters of America. In Superior Court, the judge directed a verdict of guilty. The jury said "No." The judge insisted and imposed a $5 fine and a $20 assessment for court costs on Mrs. Girodat.[1]

One month later, the Roman Catholic bishop of Albany, New York, Edmund F. Gibbons, made news by becoming the first prelate to forbid such gambling on Roman Catholic property. He announced:

> The game of bingo in this diocese has ceased to
> be a harmless pastime. Whatever financial profits it
> may yield and whatever may be said in extenuation
> of it as a diversion, it cannot escape severe censure
> as outright gambling on a large scale. It is growing
> daily. The stakes are mounting higher and the gam-
> bling fever is rising with them. . . . It is scandalizing
> the faithful and bringing contempt on religion.[2]

Within the next year there were further reactions among Roman Catholic leaders against games of chance. Archbishop Samuel Alphonsus Stritch of Milwaukee put a ban on all games of chance.[3] Bishop Henry Althoff of Belleville, Illinois, not only forbade church gambling, but voiced the hope that his people would support their churches by direct contribution rather than by parish parties and festivals. Archbishop John Joseph Glennon of St. Louis condemned gambling games as "unworthy of our Catholic people . . . causing much scandal. . . ." [4]

The crusade was not shared by all. In 1938, *Time* reported on a survey by George Gallup which revealed that half the people of the United States approved of gambling, in church or out.[5] Later, *Time* reported that out of more than two hundred Episcopal and Roman Catholic bishops, "not more than a dozen or so banned bingo as a means of raising money." [6]

In the past decade, the bingo question has become more explosive. At the present time, it is still illegal in 80 per cent of the states. Nevertheless, churches have persisted in conducting bingo. A Newark, New Jersey, clergyman claims his church has made as much as $250,000 a year on bingo. Another in Jersey City netted $100,000 a year.[7]

Today, Protestant clergymen are opposed—almost solidly— to bingo on ethical grounds. In the Roman Catholic Church, only a minority of the clergy has spoken out against the game. Other Roman Catholic priests have led the movement to legalize bingo, directing their people to vote in favor of legalizing it. In Louisiana, the superintendent of state police, Colonel Francis C. Grevemberg, went to church one Sunday for prayer and meditation, and heard himself denounced from the pulpit as "a Judas," because he had halted church bingo along with other forms of gambling in the state. His parish priest was expressing a point of view voiced by many others—that bingo is a harmless, fund-raising activity in the House of God, and to interfere is a Gestapo or MVD tactic.[8]

On April 30, 1955, a Roman Catholic priest was selling chances on an automobile on the main street of Madison, New Jersey, then the writer's home town. A member of the local Methodist Church was asked to buy a chance, and refused because it was gambling. The priest asked, "Well, what's wrong with gambling?" A business man in Madison asked the same question just two days before, when his place of business was closed for thirty days because chances were being sold on the premises. What the church is allowed to do on the street becomes an offense which closes a man's place of business when carried on in his establishment!

In 1957 the State of New York became the ninth state to legalize bingo games, and that same year New Jersey also lifted the ban on bingo. Today in New York, New Jersey, and many other states Roman Catholic churches display large signs announcing the schedule of the weekly or monthly games of chance.

What's wrong with gambling?

The nature of this investigation does not allow an extensive discussion of the evils of gambling. However, an attempt should be made to give briefly some of the principles which gambling violates, principles people should have in mind as they evaluate gambling as a money-making activity for the church.

In the first place, gambling transfers property in a way that is not acceptable to a regulated and planned order. Of the four general ways by which property can be transferred—by theft, by chance, by exchange, and by gift—the first two are illegitimate. The wrong of transferring property by theft, which includes all forms of cheating, is quite clear. Transferring property by chance, also, is wrong because it goes contrary to order, skill, reason, and intelligence.

Those who consider the matter on a superficial plane usually ask what the difference is between a gambler who takes a chance for profit and the farmer who takes a chance on the weather and on fluctuating prices. Or, they ask what the difference is between the gambler and an investor who buys stocks. Briefly, the farmer and the stockholder take *necessary* risks in the course of performing social services; the gambler takes a *created* risk and makes no social contribution in doing so. In the course of his work the farmer seeks to minimize the chances that must be taken. The gambler depends on chances; therefore, he creates them that his stakes may be higher. The game of bingo or the scheme of chance involved in raffling off a quilt creates an unnecessary risk that transfers property by chance, thus repudiating reason, art, ability, skill, intelligence, and planning.

In the second place, gambling encourages indifference toward justice and right. One who enters into games of chance is likely to become indifferent to all order and justice, as pointed out by B. Seebohm Rowntree:

> The "honour" of a confirmed gambler, even in
> high life, is known to be a very hollow commodity,
> and where there is less to lose in social esteem even
> this slender substitute for virtue is absent. The
> barrier between fraud and smartness does not exist
> for most of them.[9]

Furthermore, gambling encourages indifference toward the material interests and well-being of one's fellow man.[10] At best it is an enterprise in which one gains only as another loses. Gambling ". . . sears the sympathies, cultivates a hard egotism, and so produces a general deterioration of character." [11] In this game, all property is dealt with on a nonhuman principle, with a man trying to get something from his neighbor without making any return.

In the fourth place, gambling leads the individual into a form of mysticism that becomes a pseudo religion. In the mind of the average gambler, the superstitions of a dark age linger on. Faith in this charm ... or that event ... becomes the gambler's religion. Some gamblers study the rules of astrology to see if the roulette table is for or against the player. Certain numbers carry hidden meanings. Other individuals believe their destiny lies in a rabbit's foot, an old coin, or the color of the backs of playing cards. The gambler believes that in some unknown way the forces of Nature will direct events or movements of material things in such a way that he will profit. To determine whether Nature is going to act for him or against him, he faithfully watches the signs.[12] Hence, gambling tends to corrupt true religion; the superstitions a man embraces become his faith.

The church, by promoting lotteries, raffles, and other games of chance, has exploited a weakness in people, the weakness of wanting something for nothing. The defense has been that the money is for a "good cause." But, for good or bad, the end does not justify the means!

It is difficult—at least for this writer—to picture Jesus sending out his disciples to sell chances on a quilt! And it is even more difficult to picture him in the marketplace selling chances on a cart!

Merchandising Schemes

From an early date, at least since the fifteenth century, church socials have been held for the purpose of raising money. A great many types of money-making schemes have evolved from the church social. Although the element of giving is found to some extent, the prominent idea in these schemes is to exchange goods, services, or entertainment for money. These schemes take the form of bazaars, entertainments, church suppers, the talent plan, rummage sales, commission selling, and coupon-redemption plans.

Church Bazaars. The church bazaar is a social event in which items, generally made by the people, are sold. A partial history of the bazaar in the church can be found in *The Ladies' Home Journal* from 1903 through 1917, where a series of articles appeared in a section called "The Minister's Social Helper," dedicated to describing the latest money-raising methods. Also, two articles by William Hale in *The Forum* in 1896, collected information on 500 money-raising occasions, many associated with bazaars.

Tragically, ministers have entered into the spirit of the activity by advertising bazaars from the pulpit. A Scotch minister once announced the coming bazaar by declaring: "Weel, friends, the kirk is urgently in need o'siller, and, as we hae failed to get it honestly, we'll hae to see what like a bazaar can do for us." [13] Another minister advertised with the words, "Tis an honorable kind of thievery." [14] And another opened the bazaar saying, "You have come to be cheated, and if you have not come to be cheated a little, you deserve to be cheated a good deal." [15]

Entertainments. Associated with the bazaar are varieties of entertainments; however, church entertainments frequently are held independent of bazaars. After studying five hundred money-raising occasions, one observer expressed his concern over some of the entertainments put on by churches, leading him to conclude that "nothing could be more disturbing than a review of the list of church entertainments, public performances for money." [16]

Such a disturbing entertainment in a Missouri church concluded with this song:

> Oh! the world looks bright and our hearts are light
>   and gay,
>   We have done the very best we can do,

When a woman wills she will always find a way,
    And I'm sure you think so, too.
And now good-bye, for our entertainment's o'er.
    Our dollars are shining and bright;
Our troubles are all o'er, hard times will come no
    more,
    So we'll bid you all a fond good-night.

CHORUS:

Weep no more, dear sisters,
Oh, weep no more, I pray.
We will sing one song for the dollar we have
    begged,
Then we'll wander to our homes so far away.[17]

Church Suppers. Today the kitchen equipment is an important part of the church building. Church suppers (or dinners) are generally an important part of the bazaar, but not all suppers are associated with the bazaar. To prepare these meals, the latest kitchen equipment is found in many churches. In fact, kitchen equipment has been purchased at the expense of other facilities in church buildings.

A survey—made by the *Christian Herald* in 1932—among churches ranging in size from cathedrals to village chapels, showed the average American church served twenty meals a year, with an average guest list of 118. These results led a Mr. Haskin to the following conclusion:

> In these hard times the cookstove is as much a
> part of the average Protestant church in the United
> States as the communion rail. Over 400,000,000
> meals were cooked in 200,000 church kitchens in
> 1931. The profits paid for pews, pulpits, paint,
> and charity. They lifted mortgages and bought
> billiard balls, pipe organs, linoleum, and furnaces.
> Sometimes they also paid the preacher's salary. And
> when the pious ladies of the Aid Society weren't

cooking for money they were cooking to fill up the empty pews on Sunday and to bring folks out for the Wednesday evening prayer-meeting. There is nothing, it appears, that peps up Sunday School and church attendance like a Pot Luck Supper or a Chicken Stew. The church now travels, like an army, on its belly.[18]

The Talent Plan. In this plan each member of the congregation is given an amount of money—a "talent"—which he is to increase by some money-making project of his own. The amount given to each member varies from fifty cents to a dollar; however, one congregation in Ohio gave a ten-dollar bill to every member. This plan was advocated in 1912 by "The Minister's Social Helper," of *The Ladies' Home Journal.* Then, as now, it carried a degree of respectability because the promoters claimed it to be scriptural, based on Matthew 25:14-30.

There is something about the Talent Plan that invites publicity. For instance, in 1939 a Methodist Church in New York invited 127 persons to take a dollar bill from the offering plate and put it to work. Three months later, every bill was accounted for plus a profit of 375 per cent! [19] To the present day this plan is widely publicized in both secular and religious periodicals.

Rummage Sales. In the rummage sale, unwanted items are donated by members and friends of the congregation, to be sold at the church or from a vacant store. These sales are defended on two counts. First, it is claimed they help the poor by providing clothing at a nominal cost, and by the items' being sold (instead of given away) the receivers do not lose their self-respect. In the second place, the rummage sale can be a source of income gained at a minimum of overhead expense. An exceptional example is a church in Chicago that netted $20,000 from a single rummage sale in 1949.

There are, of course, variations of the rummage sale. One

such example is a church in New Jersey that acts as a clearing-house, having the members bring outgrown or unwanted ready-to-wear clothing to the church. The church sells the items and charges a percentage of the purchase price as a commission for selling.

Another variation is the "Parcel Post Sale," where each member is asked to send something—wrapped as a parcel post package—to the church, to be sold at a set price or at auction. The entire cost of the package is retained by the church.

An activity which falls into the same category as the rummage sale is the collecting of old paper, rags, and other unwanted goods, which, in turn, are sold to junk dealers. This was popular during World War II—because of the government's urgent calls for such items—but it was mentioned in 1913 by the editor of "The Minister's Social Helper," a column of *The Ladies' Home Journal* previously referred to. The writer expressed concern over the fact that a few of the poor men of a certain town had lost considerable income because the ladies of the local church had gone into their business of collecting old clothes, rubber, and discarded items in general.[20]

Commission Selling. In this venture, the organization buys merchandise at wholesale and sells at a profit, hence the church operates on the same basis as a retail establishment—except that it does not pay taxes, or abide by numerous other regulations applicable to a business! This type of merchandising was first mentioned by *The Ladies' Home Journal* in 1909, giving evidence it was not a practice, in a general sense, prior to 1909.

In 1949, a Methodist Church in New Jersey took advantage of the Christmas season and brought into the church a toy display on consignment, asking the members to purchase their toys through the church. The church paper for December, 1949, gave the financial report of the toy sale and concluded: "More ticket

and toy money to come in. You see when you purchase Christmas gifts at the church, it helps your church—and you!"

In some communities this practice has grown until the church
is required to obtain a license for selling. And, as long as the
church runs competition with the merchants, it is only fair that
the church should meet the same requirements as the merchants.

Coupon-Redemption Plans. The idea of this scheme is to get
church people to buy certain commodities with the assurance
that a small fraction of the cost will be turned back to the
church. In 1932, a Mr. Adolph O. Goodwin introduced and
promoted a coupon-redemption plan that literally swept the
country.

The true nature of the plan was hidden by a number of
idealistic goals. It held out the ideal of better working conditions
for laborers; manufacturers participating in the plan were expected to put into operation an ascending scale of wage increases and pay a living wage, not lower than that established
as a minimum by the government. They were to provide decent
working conditions, to refrain from employing child labor, and
to work toward conditions leading to security and permanency
of employment. A social justice committee, composed of a
Protestant, a Roman Catholic, and a Jew were to adjust complaints or direct the complaints to an arbitration committee. A
final appeal to the idealism of the church was made when Mr.
Goodwin hired between six and seven hundred people, a large
number of them being unemployed clergymen.

Behind this cloak of idealism, however, was the bare fact that
it was a plan to make money, a lot of money, for Mr. Goodwin
and his colleagues. The plan can best be understood by looking,
first, at the part played by the ladies of the churches.

A representative of the Goodwin Corporation came before
the women's society of a local church and secured the consent
of a number of competent women to act as "agents" or "broad-

casters" to stimulate the purchase of those articles listed by the corporation's catalogue. The catalogue contained every conceivable thing from a toothbrush to automobiles. But only one brand of each type of article was included. For example, Pepsodent tooth paste might be included, but not Iodent. Perhaps a Chevrolet could be purchased through the plan, but not a Ford. The list included more than a thousand articles, such as automatic pencils, radios, garters, corsets, girdles, galoshes, electric equipment, mops, roofing, gasoline, spark plugs, manicure supplies, headache remedies, insecticides, rouge, and three classes of automobiles.

Each woman who signed as an agent agreed to serve for a period of three years. Her task was to instruct ten or twelve families under her care to buy only those articles listed in the catalogue, then to save the labels or wrappers or some token of each purchase. Once a month the agent gathered the tokens and sent them to the Goodwin Corporation, who, in turn, remitted a check amounting to 2 per cent of the total purchases represented by the tokens. In reality, the church received a "kickback" of 2 per cent of all purchases made by the members.

Turning to the manufacturers' end of this scheme, it is not surprising to find them clamoring to get in on this gigantic monopoly. Of course, the manufacturers financed the whole program, since they had to agree to spend an additional 3 per cent of total volume of business in a given area on newspaper advertising. In addition, they paid 1½ per cent of the volume of church business to the Goodwin Corporation, making a total cost to the manufacturers of 6½ per cent.

When the *Christian Century* first reported on the plan, nearly 250,000 agents or broadcasters had signed. According to one estimation, at a minimum average expenditure of $5 a week per family, or $650,000,000 a year, the Goodwin Corporation stood to net approximately $10,000,000 the first year.[21] Responses were epidemic. In Buffalo 80 per cent of the Protestant and Jewish congregations signed up. Atlanta entered the plan 90 per cent strong. In Denver ten out of eleven churches came through. Bishops of all denominations approved.

What happened? Strong protests were raised by some religious publications, especially the *Christian Century,* pointing to the plan as a wide-scale monopoly. The eyes of church leaders were opened to the evils of the plan; nevertheless, it continued to be promoted by various groups. For instance, a similar plan known as "The Christian Herald Church Help Plan" was introduced by the *Christian Herald* in 1949. It was discontinued after only one year, but in its short period of duration, more than 10,000 churches were enrolled.

Throughout the history of these merchandising schemes, objections have been raised about their competition with the businessmen of the community. Often, the businessman pays in two ways—first, he is asked to donate items; second, he loses his potential customers to the church. The pressures that are brought to bear on the merchant, in some cases, border on blackmail!

Another serious danger of these social activities is their tendency to become a substitute for offerings, a salve for the conscience.

There is also the question whether a tax-exempt institution should be allowed to run competition with individuals or establishments which are subject to taxation. Some cities and states currently are wrestling with this question. A case in point is Richmond, Virginia, where on March 31, 1955, attorney J. Elliott Drinard held that St. Paul's Episcopal Church, in making Lenten meals available to the public at a price was liable for the food license tax under Section 10-105 of the city license tax ordinance. Six of the nine Richmond City Councilmen introduced a bill to exempt from city license requirements church food sales. It was passed; but the new exemption is limited by state constitutional provisions, which provide that the sales must take place on church property and the revenue used for religious purposes. Another question raised was whether the church could claim exemption from real estate taxes if the property is not used exclusively for religious worship.[22]

The strongest case against these schemes is the witness of the Church before the world. In her message, the Church claims to have the greatest news that ever has come to mankind. She proclaims a message of abundant and eternal life through her risen Lord; yet, she advertises her bazaars and fairs before the public as though these activities were her only hope of remaining in existence. In affirmations of faith individual Christians say "I believe . . ."—but, evidently, that faith is not strong enough to make the necessary sacrifices in order that the Church might continue to be the visible Body of Christ.

Church Farm and Lord's Acre

In the contemporary rural church there has developed a method of support similar to the early glebe, namely, the church farm. It has three definite variations. The first is for the pastor to cultivate a small farm—called "The Pastor's Homestead"— in addition to his ministerial duties. In the second variation, the members of the congregation cultivate the land and the proceeds go to the church. In the third variation, a church owns a farm and leases it, with the church receiving the rent or share-payments.

Some pastors speak favorably of the "homestead" plan, contending that a small farm for the pastor will encourage longer tenure, bring him closer to his people, and give him a degree of financial independence.

The church farm, operated by the congregation, provides an opportunity for group participation, and can give considerable support—as much as $20,000 or $30,000 a year. On the negative side of the ledger is the fear of landlordism.

The Lord's Acre—in its inception—was a method of church support by an individual or a family who set aside a part of a crop, livestock, or produce for the Lord's work. In recent years many innovations have been incorporated into this plan.

This plan began to take on the characteristics of a movement in 1930 when the Rev. Dumont Clarke became head of the religious department of the Farmers' Federation, Asheville, North Carolina, and directed six churches of three denominations in the Lord's Acre plan. The results of the first year were so successful that fifty churches made use of the plan the following year. Since then a growing number of churches have been using some form of the plan.

One recent innovation is the so-called Lord's Hour plan. Or, similar to this is the Vocational Giving plan. Both plans have the same central idea—the giving of an hour's wage or portion of salary at the beginning of each day, week, or month. In a South Carolina church the mill workers give a day's pay each month. In a Florida church the people who do not work the soil or raise livestock are asked to give part of their income as their Lord's Acre project. Consequently, some give the first hour's wage each week; a storekeeper gives the largest day's sale during the year; a saleslady gives the greatest week's profit; and a seamstress gives the proceeds from sewing for a certain period of time.

In the depression days, when the Lord's Acre plan was conceived, it was "tailor-made." Likewise, in mission fields where business still is done on the barter basis the plan has merit. Materially speaking, it has been the means of saving many rural churches. In each annual report of the Farmers' Federation, Mr. Clarke gave page after page of testimonies from pastors and laymen, enumerating the material blessings their churches received from the plan. In addition, the people themselves have been blessed. To wit—it has encouraged diversified farming; it has given meaning to the vocation of farming; and it has brought a higher standard of living to the people.

In a study of 137 Lord's Acre plans, pastors were asked to indicate the greatest values of the plan. There were 61 per cent who felt it taught stewardship; 48 per cent indicated it spiritualized farm life; 43 per cent felt it helped to make the Harvest Festival of Thanksgiving a reality; and other values high on the list were a renewed interest in tithing, prayer, church attendance, and increased membership.[23]

Nearly all the literature emphasizes the plan as a supplement to giving. This at once raises the question: is this extra to come directly or indirectly out of one's total income? If it is to come out of one's total income, then it is likely to defeat planned giving. Candidly, it appears to be another practice for getting a little more money from the people; it evades proportionate giving of one's entire income. The basic issue persists—is the Church to be supported by a dedicated proportion of the Christian's income? Or, is the Christian to go out and earn money for the church?

Another question must also be faced—how far can we go in supporting the church with produce when we are living in a cash economy? In a cash economy, it might be an evasion of one's responsibility in stewardship to try to turn back the clock to a barter system. Undoubtedly, living under a cash economy demands a great deal more discipline.

Business Enterprises

Three significant enterprises, of a business nature, not discussed previously, deserve some attention: (1) revenue-producing real estate, (2) bonds, and (3) insurance.

Revenue-Producing Urban Property. This is a commercial venture in which a congregation builds a building to provide apartments or office space. The rental income helps to meet the total church budget. Some city churches have been in a favored position for this kind of arrangement, since they own property that is extremely valuable and ideally located for business purposes. During the year when New York first felt the depression of the 1930's, the First Reformed Church contracted to receive for the first twenty-one years of a lease an average rental of $14,000 annually. The Madison Avenue Baptist Church was to receive $30,000 in annual rentals.

One of the biggest undertakings of this nature was the Baptist Temple, Rochester, New York, where in 1925 a $2,500,000 building was financed by floating a $1,000,000 first-mortgage loan by obtaining $260,000 in pledges (less than $150 per member) and by arranging for a second mortgage of $260,000. The first three floors of the fourteen-story building included the church nave, social rooms, and retail stores, and these floors were expected to produce a net annual income of $48,000— enough to retire the debt in twenty years.[24]

The danger here is the same as that of any other form of endowment, namely, that the income might become a substitute for giving on the part of the members. Again, the question of taxation appears. These churches pay real estate taxes and income taxes on that part of the building which is used commercially—but many people question the practice of a tax-exempt institution's taking advantage of a valuable downtown property in this way.

Sale of Church Bonds. Many churches are issuing bonds, paying a small interest rate—usually two or three per cent lower than an established bonding company—issued in various denominations and presumably backed by the value of the church property. The practice is defended on the premise that the members of a congregation should be willing to loan money to the church at little or no interest.

The plan is vulnerable. In the first instance, a church bond seldom represents true value. Theoretically, the property should guarantee the value of the bond; actually, however, the bond is backed by the annual income of the church. To issue bonds in this manner may manifest great faith, but it does not represent sound business—and sound business has a place in the contemporary church.

Then, too, there is always the possibility of putting the bondholders on the proverbial spot, especially if the church should come to hard times. The bondholder might be looked upon as a Shylock demanding his pound of flesh, if he desires his payment. Also, subtle pressures can be brought to bear on bondholders to overlook the interest as it comes due. It happened in Illinois when—after three years—the officials were pleased to announce that not a single investor had clipped the interest coupons, and these unclipped coupons amounted to $10,000! Many investors can afford to forget their interest, but there may be others who depend on the interest for their support. Yet, they are apt to be victims of this subtle pressure to "forget it."

Endowment Insurance. Like the church bond method, this plan provides a way for individuals to make cash payments to the church which are a combination of gift and loan. Instead of receiving interest, as in the church bond, the investor receives an endowment life insurance policy. The first step involves the formation of a trust fund by the members of a congregation. Next, each member of the fund agrees to loan money to the fund. Then, the fund becomes the source from which the congregation draws the money it needs.

In order to guarantee the repayment of this borrowed money, the church takes out an endowment life insurance policy on each investor, paying the premiums out of the annual budget, usually for a twenty-year period.

At first glance, there seems to be no vulnerable spot in this method; however, closer examination raises certain questions. The line between the principle of exchange and benevolence is blurred, since a "loan" in this case is partly a gift and partly a purchase. One of the reasons for the success of this plan is the fact that 70 per cent of the individual's investment is a gift.

For example, in the Columbian Plan (operated by the Columbian Mutual Life Insurance Company, Boston, Massachusetts) an individual pays $2,000 for a $3,000 endowment policy, maturing in thirty-five years. No dividends are received by the insured. If, on the other hand, one were to purchase a single premium or paid-up thirty-five year endowment policy worth $3,000 with a standard insurance company—such as New York Life—it would cost only $1,707. This policy would return in dividends and interest $1,104, making the net cost only $603— 30 per cent less than the Columbian Plan.

A second factor is this—it actually puts a first mortgage on the church, with the subscribers corporately holding the mortgage. To guarantee the payment of the premium by the church, a trust agreement is executed between the trustees of the loan fund and the church.

One of the selling points of this plan constitutes a serious objection. Generally, it is pointed out that the church will have a decreasing burden in paying the annual premiums due to the death of some persons prior to the completion of the thirty-five year period. It is unfortunate that a church should enter into a plan in which it makes a financial gain every time a member dies.

A final possible drawback to this plan is the practice of placing the payment of insurance premiums into the hands of the church. If the church were to fail to pay the premiums, the people would lose their insurance.

Activity and Faith

It is difficult to state, in a few words, a conclusion to a chapter as diversified as this one. In any event, some observations about the relationship between activity and personal faith are necessary at this point. This relationship can be classified—to some extent—by classifying church activity into three categories. First, there is that kind of activity which is related directly to the witnessing of one's faith—preaching, teaching, singing in the choir, serving on boards and committees, and parish visiting.

The second category is those activities which save the church money. For example, instead of the church's having to buy ready-made choir gowns, a certain group might undertake the project. The third kind of activity involves the exchange of services or products for money. Merchandising schemes fall into this category, and it is here that the church has been most vulnerable.

Throughout this chapter the point has been made, frequently, that nothing should be allowed to become a substitute for giving a dedicated portion of one's income to the work of Christ through the church. Such a substitution is a constant temptation. Another more subtle temptation is to substitute activity in the church for Christian witnessing. Many church members spend more time advertising the bazaar than telling of the wonders of Christ. They expend more energy selling tickets to an entertainment than they do in witnessing. Being active in a bazaar booth is a poor substitute for Christian service or giving.

But even this discussion is evading the basic issue. Our money-making activities do not arise from a primary desire or need for being active. Rather, they are forced upon us because the church needs money! And, tragically, we have been either unwilling to discover God's plan or else, if his plan is known, we have been unwilling to accept it.

It has become apparent to many leaders in the church that the Every Member Canvass is the most ideal method known today for the providing of gifts from Christians. Its whole structure, as outlined in the next chapter, is commendable.

X

Every Member
Canvass

The Every Member Canvass had its roots in the old subscription system, and grew out of a number of significant innovations during the early part of the twentieth century. As the
churches began to face the problems of the pew-rent system, the
multiple money-making activities, and the increasing number of
special appeals by both church and nonchurch groups, a re-
thinking of church finance was considered necessary.

Consequently, denominational boards, instead of appealing
individually to the congregations, organized to present a unified
appeal. This move toward united promotion took place in some
denominations—Methodist and Presbyterian—early in the century; others have adopted it since that time. This united appeal
encouraged congregations and national denominations to eliminate some of their special appeals and to include all askings in
one or two budgets. Out of these needs and developments has
come the Every Member Canvass.

The Every Member Canvass is a carefully planned program
whereby a congregation seeks to provide funds to meet local and
benevolent needs by a thorough visitation of the membership.
It is known by a variety of names. The United Lutherans speak
of it as the *Every Member Visit,* the Evangelical and Reformed
call it *Kingdom Roll Call,* and the American Baptists use the
term *Every Member Enlistment.*

The more significant phases of this program are (1) budgets, (2) education and promotion, (3) pledges, (4) envelopes, (5) youth participation, (6) secondary accomplishments, and (7) professional fund raisers.

Budgets

Three general types of budgets have been developed—the multiple budget, the dual-unified budget, and the single-unified budget.

The multiple budget is really the sum total of a number of budgets which have been set up by the various organizations within a congregation. Each organization sets up its own budget, based on its needs and the needs which it intends to help meet. Thus, it is conceivable that within a congregation, the Sunday School, Women's Association, Youth Group, Men's Brotherhood, and Missionary Society might have budgets independent of one another and independent of the central budget of the congregation.

The dual-unified budget brings all the financial needs under two headings—local and benevolent. Here is a case in which there are actually two separate budgets, unified by the program and emphasis of the congregation. Duplex envelopes, separate or duplex pledge cards, and separate treasurers, although not inherent, are frequently characteristics of the dual-unified budget.

The single-unified budget is one budget which provides for all the financial needs of the congregation and organizations of the congregation, both local and benevolent. If pledges are made, the individual makes only one pledge, and if envelopes are used, the single pocket envelope is most appropriate.

In comparing these three systems there is little to be said for the multiple budget. It makes the individual a victim of the appeals of every organization within the congregation; it allows for no central control or guidance of funds; it opens the way for much duplication; financial reports to the contributors seldom are made; and when the organizations offer packets of envelopes —as they often do—the individual might have four or five sets of offering envelopes.

Both the dual-unified and single-unified budgets have merits. They tend to eliminate the multiple financial appeals from the pulpit; they keep the finances of the congregation in better perspective, that is, finance is less apt to dominate the congregational program; they inform each giver of the financial needs at the beginning of the year; they enable the congregation to administer more justly the available funds; and, at the close of the year, they make it possible for the congregation to give a clear report of all financial transactions.

As for the comparative merits of these two unified budgets, each has its advocates. One might, for example, contend that the single-unified system helps to advance the idea that the church has but one program with a variety of phases; another might reply that the separation of local and benevolent budgets emphasizes the church's task abroad as well as at home. Also, the single-unified budget advocates might declare that the church as a whole should administer all funds; on the other hand, those who hold to the dual-unified system believe there is merit in allowing the individual member to appropriate his gift between local operating expenses and benevolence.

Whatever the comparative merits may be, the fact is—the budget (dual or single) has become an important phase of the Every Member Canvass.

Education and Promotion

The most modern methods are being employed as a means of educating and promoting church finance in connection with the Every Member Canvass. In addition to traditional sermons and church school lessons, the twentieth-century church makes use of plays, movies, filmstrips, turnover charts, recordings, and radio.

A significant innovation has been the co-operative effort of a number of denominations to conduct the Every Member Canvass simultaneously, thus having the benefit of greater educational and promotional means, such as newspapers, radio, and TV.

Local congregations use letters—longhand, printed, mimeographed—along with printed materials provided by denominational stewardship departments. Also popular is the congregational dinner, used to inform, educate, and inspire the members about the financial needs.

The "turnover chart" has become a useful tool in the visitation. Constructed in the form of a large tablet with a spiral binding it will stand on a table while the visitor turns the pages, telling progressively the program of the denomination and emphasizing the responsibility each member should assume for the financial needs of the church. The turnover chart was used for the first time in 1949 by at least two denominations, with a growing number making wide use of it in more recent years.

The United Lutherans, on two occasions, have provided 14-month calendars for every family, to be used from November—when the annual visitation is usually conducted—through the next December. The calendar uses each month to stress one area of the church's witness, and allows space under each date for noting church appointments.

Pledges

Not all denominations agree on the merits of individual financial pledges. Nor is there complete agreement within the denominations. However, the practice of asking each member to make a definite pledge to the church has been associated with the Every Member Canvass.

This phase of the program most nearly resembles the early subscription list method. Today, however, instead of circulating a paper on which each individual indicates his pledge or subscription, individual cards are mailed or delivered in person to the members.

A considerable amount of thought has gone into the wording of the pledge cards. The wording attempts to make clear the fact that the pledge is not legally binding. So, the Congregational Christian Church has a pledge card with the terminology, "Declaration of Intention." The Presbyterian U.S. Church has a card that reads, "In grateful recognition of God's blessings, I welcome the privilege to dedicate . . ." Another card of the Presbyterian U.S. Church merely states, "I'll give weekly . . ." Another Congregational Christian Church card reads, "Out of gratitude to God for His gifts to me I make this contribution toward. . . ." One of the United Lutheran pledge cards is briefly worded and asks for one's weekly pledge to the church "locally and throughout the world."

Terminology is important. It often makes the difference between a person's pledging or not pledging. Parenthetically, however, it might be added, a "pledge" to a church has been declared legally binding by the courts.

If there is anything in the modern Every Member Canvass which resembles former compulsory methods, it is the emphasis on pledging. In defending pledging, the advocates point to an individual's agreement to pay the butcher, the baker, and the grocer, concluding, therefore, that it is only natural that one pledge to the church. That is a poor comparison, since no man agrees to pay a specfic amount for a whole year (in advance) unless he has contracted a debt. Circumstances throughout the year partially determine what an individual will pay for bread, meat, or fuel.

Also, the advocates of pledging claim the church cannot embark upon a year unless the budget is underwritten, and it can only be underwritten if the members pledge it. Such is not the case. Many congregations operate without budget, and have done so for years.

The final argument for the pledge system is that the individual is more likely to "pay up" if he has made a pledge. This is true. But this pressure robs from the voluntary principle. Whenever the church has tried to compel the faithful to give, whether by civil or ecclesiastical laws, it has alienated the people from itself. If a man's vision broadens during the year, he should be free to increase his giving; likewise, if financial reverses or unseen demands make it necessary, he should feel free to decrease his giving.

Envelopes

There are two main reasons for using envelopes. First, for the convenience of the individual contributor; and, second, it provides the church a check on the source of each gift. The envelope is especially important when the system calls for pledges, for, if the individual contributes by cash, the envelope is the only way the treasurer or financial secretary can keep a record of the giving.

There are two primary types of church envelopes—the single and the duplex. The single is designed for a single-unified budget and the duplex for a dual-unified budget. In the single envelope system the congregation makes the final decision as to what percentage of each gift is to go to benevolence, but in using the duplex envelope the individual has authority to designate the amount he wishes to go for local work and the amount he would have go to benevolences.

A further value of the envelope system is that an envelope makes every coin or bill a gift. This is especially important with children. One child may make a greater sacrifice by bringing ten cents than another who might bring a quarter. Yet, without the use of envelopes the individual who brings the quarter thereby draws attention to himself. Of course, this same observation is true of adults, too.

Youth Participation

In recent years the denominations have begun to realize the importance of educating children and youth in stewardship. This, also, is a break with the past, since in former generations the head of the house usually made the family's contribution, with giving by children confined to pennies for Sunday School.

Today, through young people's groups, the children and youth are being informed of the total financial program of the church and are given an opportunity to take part in the Every Member Canvass. In some denominations the youth actually carry out their own canvass. One such case is the "Youth Budget" plan of the United Presbyterian Church, U.S.A. Another is the Baptist Youth Fellowship Sharing Plan of the American Baptist Convention, emphasizing service, evangelistic activity, and giving of material possessions.

Promotional literature of the United Lutheran Church includes a special youth paper, entitled, *Stewart the Steward,* which carries stewardship items in news form and cartoon form. In one year the theme was "How Far Can I Reach?" It reminded the youth that although one could not reach far, yet, by holding hands with one another, as a group they could reach into every area of the church's life.

The Church of God discovered an interesting approach to children as well as to adults. To raise the benevolence budget in full it was calculated that it would cost $2 to carry the entire load for one minute. Any child giving $2 or more, therefore, actually supported the entire benevolent program for one minute, and was called a "Minute Man." Pins and ribbons were prepared, labeling the child a "Minute Man" or indicating the number of minutes he carried the program.

Usually, in participating in youth budget plans, the youth and children of a local congregation accept as their responsibility a certain amount or percentage of the congregational budget, organize into committees, inform and educate the various groups in the Church School regarding the plan, approach every child and young person for a pledge, and then issue envelopes.

Thus, the churches are beginning to assume a long-neglected phase of stewardship-youth participation. In the manual for canvassers in the Evangelical and Reformed Church there is given the following answer to those who believe only the man of the house is to make the subscription and gift:

> A subscription has a relation to religion,
> rather than to finances, and every member of the
> family should have a personal interest in and
> connection with the church through a separate
> subscription. You do not commune for your wife.
> You do not attend church for the children. You
> do not do their praying or Bible reading. Each
> one is a member of the church and should enroll
> as a subscriber and have the joy of giving.

Secondary Accomplishments

It is becoming quite common for some churches to use the machinery and organization of the Every Member Canvass to carry out projects which are not confined to the financial program. Some denominations use the Every Member Canvass to get people to subscribe to the denominational paper. Others use it for evangelism.

Literature is suggesting people be informed—in the course of a canvass—of the possibilities of including the church in their wills. Also, pledge cards are being provided to allow the pledging of time and talents to the church. During a building program, congregations have made every-member visits to keep the membership informed of the progress.

Professional Fund Raisers

The activities of professional fund raisers have spread rapidly, and their technique is basically an Every Member Canvass. It cannot be denied that these firms are successful in raising money. In many cases, they have raised more money than the church expected to raise.

They have grown in demand because many churches without professional help have failed to reach their goals. A survey for the Philadelphia Council of Churches showed this picture of defeat. Church campaigns in that area with a total goal of $5,000,000 obtained only $3,500,000 when no professional help was used.

Professional fund raisers employ men with wide business experience. Their personnel are highly paid. Their approach to a campaign is scientific. They know approximately how much money they can expect to raise and from whom it will come. They know what kind of publicity to emphasize and how many volunteers will be needed for the canvass. They are highly efficient.

Two questions are raised as to the over-all advisability of using these concerns. First, is it sound, financially, to pay the cost of the professional fund raiser? Thousands of congregations have answered in the affirmative. Put strictly on an immediate financial basis, there is no question about it; the overhead cost is more than offset by the additional funds raised.

The second question concerns the long-range effect of a campaign on the life and witness of the church. This depends upon the firms and their various motivational procedures. One firm employs social pressure by asking each individual to make public his subscription. Such a technique was employed in the colonial period, but it still comes under the condemnation of Jesus when he says: "Do not your alms before men."

Sound business has a place in the church. And the church should be free to call for help from the business world. Where the church has done this, budgets have been oversubscribed and the cost of new buildings underwritten. Nevertheless, there is something lacking in the spiritual life of the church when secular professional money raisers have to be employed. One's giving should be a manifestation of his faith, and it seems to be a reflection on the church that the faith it proclaims has not produced the necessary funds for maintaining and extending her program.

Some of the professional fund raisers have brought a spiritual note into the church, and for this the church can be thankful. But, one wonders whether the next step is to hire professional recruiters to build up the church membership!

XI

Motives
for Giving

Why does one give to the church? It is difficult to answer this question objectively, for it is not easy to "know thyself." Yet, the ultimate worth of any gift is to be found in the motive behind the gift. As a man "thinketh in his heart, so is he." [1] It would seem that the measure of a man is not so much in what he does or says, but rather in what he intends. The Lord of the Church said, "There is nothing covered that shall not be revealed; and hid, that shall not be known." [2] In the light of that statement, the following conclusion might well be made: *Be sure your motives will find you out.*

Throughout the previous chapters the motives of giving have been as apparent as the methods. In fact, one's motivation probably is more significant than the particular method that may be employed. Therefore, as an attempt is made to move in the direction of a philosophy of Christian stewardship, a restatement of the several motives which have been manifested in the distant past will be helpful, along with an evaluation of some contemporary motives for giving.

Oblation and Fear

"For by grace are ye saved through faith; and that not of yourselves: it is the gift of God: Not of works, lest any man should boast." [3] This declaration is like a watershed which divides the New Testament message of redemption from all implications that God's love and forgiveness are dependent upon man's good works. "Just as I am, without one plea, in my hands no price I bring. . . ." That is the basis on which a Christian comes to God for forgiveness.

Oblation. In spite of this declaration, men often have been led to give to the church in order to help assure their salvation. Believing their gifts would help bring salvation to them and their families, landowners endowed the church with their property. When the Mass took the place of the Lord's Supper, the oblation motive for giving was encouraged even more. It was this motivation that opened the way for abuses in the sale of indulgences, the adoration of relics, and the pilgrimages to holy places. These practices—which grew out of the oblation motive— sparked the Protestant Reformation. To the present day, even in Protestant churches, people are moved to give because they believe it will help bring them salvation. A questionnaire circulated among thousands of people, listing thirty-five reasons for giving to the church, turned up a considerable percentage who indicated they gave to help pay their debt to God.

In moving toward a philosophy of Christian stewardship, this one theme needs to be sounded again and again—"In my hands no price I bring, simply to thy cross I cling"; and "For by grace are ye saved. . . ."

On which side of the Cross are we living? This is the basic question. On the other side of the Cross, Paul—whose name was then Saul—was striving for salvation by way of the righteousness of the Law. On this side of the Cross, his devotion to goodness was a devotion to Christ, and this was a response, not a proposition. The case might be stated by asking on which side of Wittenberg Martin Luther is speaking. Before he began to study and to teach the New Testament at Wittenberg, his acts of devotion were performed in order that he might be saved.

But after discovering this watershed of justification by faith, his good acts were responses to God's love in Christ. Likewise, we might ask on which side of Aldersgate John Wesley is speaking. Before his heartwarming experience his acts of goodness were human efforts to find the "peace of God." But, after this experience, his entire life was a response, as he wrote, "I felt I did trust in Christ, Christ alone for salvation; and an assurance was given me that He had taken away my sins, even mine, and saved me from the law of sin and death." There is an eternity of difference between acting to gain merit and acting in response to the gift of salvation through Jesus Christ.

Motive of Fear. The motive of fear in some cases is related closely to the oblation motive, for it has been the fear of hell and purgatory that has moved some people to give. However, people also have given out of fear for what God might do to them if they were unfaithful. In the past, some people have tithed out of fear, as the strain from the early English rhyme indicates:

> For lambe, pig and calf, and for other the like,
> Tithe so as thy cattle the Lord do not strike.[4]

Needless to say, such motivation has no place in a Christian philosophy of stewardship; the motive must come from love, a love that casteth out all fear.

Legal Compulsion

During the Middle Ages—in England and on the Continent—the laws of the state and the church required citizens to support the church. Although the principles of the Reformation called for voluntary support of the church, the reformers generally turned to civil powers to collect church support. Especially in England, a man either paid the church rate on Sunday or the police would collect it by force the following week. Also, in

America, certain churches were established by and enjoyed the hand of the civil law. It is well to remind ourselves that people have been put in jail and their goods confiscated because they failed to pay their church dues—in America!

History could repeat itself, if the separation of church and state is not maintained. Love never can be subject to the compulsion of civil law. Thus, compulsory giving is completely out of harmony with Christian stewardship. Each man is to give what his heart and mind would have him give, "and not do it reluctantly or under compulsion." [5]

Personal Glorification

It is quite possible that men always have been motivated to give because of the personal prestige which was assured. This motive was worked extensively in the early American church where, in the pew-rent system, a man's social position was indicated by the pew he occupied. Also, the subscription list enabled the larger giver to gain recognition. Today, when individual gifts are made public there is always the danger of motivating men by the element of personal prestige.

Jesus condemned such motivation whenever he saw the religious men of his day parade their goodness. The Christian is not to seek recognition either by sounding a trumpet in the marketplace or by having his name appear at the head of the list. Rather, he is to give in such a way that the left hand does not even know what the right hand is doing.[6]

Personal Profit

When a man conducts his financial affairs on a Christian basis, he is likely to prosper. And, it is very possible that many men are prosperous today because they have run their business as though Christ were a member of the firm. Many men have testified to this, and the church can rejoice in these testimonies.

However, when a man is motivated to take Christ as a member of the firm in order to become more prosperous, Christ is not being glorified: he is being exploited.

In the past fifty years, a number of men have claimed tithing has brought them material blessings. The question is not, Is the claim correct? Rather, the question is, Can personal gain be a valid Christian motive for giving? Thomas Kane probably did more than any other man to advance the thesis that tithing brings material prosperity. Yet, he did not advocate tithing for this reason. In 1870, he began to tithe his income. After five years he noticed his business had undergone a decided change for the better. Thereupon, he began making personal inquiries regarding the temporal prosperity of those who tithed, and found almost complete agreement among tithers—tithing pays!

Kane then wrote a tract on the subject and sent it to at least three-fourths of all the evangelical ministers in the United States. With the tract went a circular saying:

> My belief is that God blesses in temporal as well
> as spiritual things the man who honours Him by
> setting apart a stated portion of his income to His
> service. I have never known an exception—have
> you? [7]

Over a period of ten years Mr. Kane sent out more than 5,000,000 tracts and pamphlets on this subject. More than forty years later, he wrote a short pamphlet stating he had received thousands of replies to the question above, with less than a dozen indicating they thought they were exceptions. He says, "In most instances the writers seemed to think that tithing was a kind of insurance against even temporary financial loss." [8]

It was the promise of material blessings that led the Mormons to adopt tithing more widely at the turn of the century. In the spring of 1899, Utah had gone through two years of drought. Lorenzo Snow, president of the church, visited St. George in southern Utah and spoke to the Mormons on tithing. He compared the people with Israel in the day of Malachi and promised the Mormons rain would come, if they would pay their tithes. The people obeyed, not only in St. George, but all over the church, as the president continued his appeals for obedience to "the commandment of God."

Weeks passed. The hot winds blew. The crops wilted. Then, one morning in August, a telegram was laid on the president's desk—"Rain in St. George." The creeks and rivers filled, and crops matured. Although the Mormons previously had held that tithing was expected of the faithful, it was the experience of 1899 that brought the practice into almost universal use among them.[9]

In the twentieth century this belief in material rewards and success from tithing has become widespread. A good share of the books on tithing include illustrations revealing a belief in God's reward to the tither. Some have gone so far as to say that even the unbeliever would experience material benefits and success if he were to set aside a tenth of his income for others.[10] Some of the testimonies follow.

Charles Page was down to his last dollar when a Salvation Army girl assured him he would prosper if he would tithe. He did better, he gave her fifteen cents. Then, he went to Tulsa, Oklahoma—and struck oil! It was almost fantastic the way he was successful in striking oil consistently nearly every time he drilled. Various writers have quoted him as giving the secret to his success as follows: "I think I've missed only two holes in my life. You see, I couldn't miss; I was in partnership with the Big Fellow and He made geology." [11]

Another case is a man whose business failed with debts of more than $100,000. He opened his Bible to Genesis 28:22 and, drawing a pencil mark around that verse, said, "From this moment on as long as I live, of all that God gives me I will give

Him a tenth." Not long afterward he called on an old friend, a physician, who gave him a recipe for a lotion. He began to manufacture it and, in a few years, became the president of one of America's most successful manufacturing companies.[12]

Or, consider the case of a Southern lawyer who began his practice by adopting the principle of tithing. In a certain year, he made $3,900; the next year he made $5,303; the next $21,451; and the next year his income more than doubled when he earned $55,455. The year in which he first related his belief in tithing he earned $75,862.[13]

The success stories have not been confined to men of great wealth. Books designed for the average layman give case after case of people in modest circumstances who prospered because they started tithing. One young man who was assured things would turn out better if he tithed gave it a try. He later said:

> You know, that thing is almost spooky—the way
> God has made good, the minute I came across. . . .
> Shortly after the middle of the month, a policy
> carrying a premium much more than the tenth,
> dropped down on me out of the clouds, figuratively
> speaking. It was a thing I had no idea of getting—
> no right to expect, and you won't ever have to
> argue with me again as to whether God does make
> good His blessed promises.[14]

The "Biblical Wheat" experiment, conducted by Perry Hayden, emphasizes the material rewards of tithing. Throughout the accounts of this adventure it is brought out that God prospers those who tithe, and that he also shows special care for crops that are being tithed. Mr. Hayden claims his own personal experience verified this.

When his mill was in the hands of its creditors in 1936 Perry Hayden kept on tithing. He even increased his giving to 15 per cent the following year. By the end of 1937 the business was out of debt, and by 1938 a new warehouse had to be erected. Hayden stated in 1947 that the mill was running day and night and the business had increased 300 per cent between 1937 and 1947.[15]

Mr. R. G. LeTourneau, who is well-known for his faith in the power of tithing, once stated:

> The minute I started my partnership with God, business boomed. The next year my sales were over $100,000. The second year over $150,000. The third year over $200,000. Then we hit almost $400,000. It kept going like that, in leaps and bounds. In 1939 our sales were over $7,000,000; later, $40,000,000.[16]

It is not at all surprising that many firmly believe tithing brings material prosperity. According to the Bible, faithfulness in giving and prosperity go hand in hand. One of the undated leaflets published by the Layman Company indicates that of the 72 biblical references to giving, 48 show open promises of God's blessing to the giver.[17]

As indicated at the beginning of this discussion, it is not the purpose here to determine whether or not tithing brings material gain. In fact, the writer is inclined to believe it does. If it were for no other reason, the discipline of tithing compels one to handle his financial affairs in a businesslike manner, and this in itself helps to bring financial prosperity. It is a purpose of this study, however, to examine the validity of making material prosperity a motivation for giving to Christ and his church.

Tithing might help a man gain the whole world, but if his reason for tithing is to gain the world, he can be sure the world is all he will gain.

It hardly can be questioned that the promise of material blessings had a great deal to do with the spread of the idea of the Lord's Acre plan in the early 1930's. As early as 1924 the

Georgia ministers and farmers who had used the plan were claiming the acres devoted to the Lord produced better crops than were produced on surrounding acres. Where the crop was cotton, the crops had been less smitten by the boll weevil.[18] Dauss King, one of the first farmers in Georgia to sign up for the Lord's Acre project, reported: "The acre I planted for the Lord produced a bale of fine cotton, while farmers in my neighborhood lost virtually all their crop from the boll weevil."

Six Bluffton, Georgia, church members signed tracts for the Baptist Association in which they claimed they had prospered above the average of their community. One of these, J. E. Shaw, said his Lord's Acre escaped the boll weevil completely. Some men claimed to have counted the bolls on cotton plants in two adjoining fields, one containing a Lord's Acre and the other an ordinary field, reporting the plants on the Lord's Acre had 59 bolls of cotton and the other had but 21. The Rev. Mr. Melton answered all inquiries by saying, "It is clearly obvious that the Lord helped to give the farmers splendid crops on the land planted in His name." [19]

These reports were not confined to the South. In Carver, Massachusetts, a Baptist Church undertook a financial need by asking for the use of a cranberry bog for one year. "God's bog," as it was called, was donated by Mrs. Annie S. Boardway. She confessed it was the poorest quarter-section on her property, but the minister, the Rev. Charles W. Hidden, wanted it to be the poorest so that the demonstration would be more obvious. Throughout the growing season "God's bog" withstood the usual ravages suffered by the cranberry plant. Early in the summer a terrific windstorm swept over Carver, uprooting trees and damaging many of the cranberry bogs in its path. Although "God's bog" lay in the direct line of the storm, it came through unharmed. Then came the ravages of the fire worms and other bog pests, and again the quarter-section was spared. During the first week in September sharp frosts descended on the district. It had been a dry year, and the streams had dried up, so there was no way of flooding the bogs to save them. Badly scared, the cranberry growers started early to salvage as many of the berries as was possible. The Rev. Mr. Hidden remained calm and advised the people not to worry, for God would provide the means for saving the crop. Within the next few days there came a generous rain, and the crop was saved. "God's bog" yielded 100 per cent more berries that year, and the berries were bigger and better than ever had been grown on that bog. To all this, Mr. Hidden replied, "I had no fear of making this test. It was made in absolute faith, and the results show clearly, to me at least, that God has not failed his believing servant." [20]

In the "Biblical Wheat" experiment the claim was made that God took special care of the dedicated wheat. It began on September 26, 1940, when Mr. Hayden planted a cubic inch of wheat on a small plot of land donated for the purpose by Henry Ford. A tithe of the harvest of fifty cubic inches was given to the church and the remaining forty-five cubic inches were planted the following year. This was continued every year through 1946; the harvest that year was 75,000 bushels of wheat valued at $150,000.[21]

Pheasants threatened the "Biblical Wheat" project in 1942, but the planters refused to panic; instead, they recalled the promise of Malachi 3:11, "And I will rebuke the devourer for your sakes, and he shall not destroy the fruits of your ground." With hunting season to open in five days, they knew the Lord would take care of the pheasants. Later the craw of one of the pheasants—shot near the field—was opened, and it was found that only white wheat had been eaten by the bird; the "biblical wheat" was red wheat.[22]

Are these claims of divine favor a valid motive for Christian giving? There are accounts in the Bible where man has bargained with God and has promised to tithe if God would bless him. Jacob, for instance, made a bargain with God, promising he would give God a tenth of all that God had given him, if he were permitted to return to his father's home in safety and peace.[23]

Such bargaining has no place in the worship and devotion of a Christian. The Christian has been bought with a price, a price so great that it dwarfs any barter he might offer. It is true, the Israelite was urged to give because God had redeemed him from Egypt and had given him the land which flowed with milk and honey. But this was a response of gratitude, not one side of a bargain. Likewise, the Christian is urged to give because he has been redeemed by the blood of Christ and has received the gift of all gifts, even Jesus Christ.

If a man is moved to tithe or to set aside an acre of land for the Lord because he believes it will bring him prosperity, he can look upon the transaction as a "deal" or a "proposition." Tithing can be considered a gift only if it is given with no strings attached.

Self-Interest

The promotional propaganda and the slogans for benevolent work consistently emphasize the selfish motive. A national example is the Marshall Plan, which had to be justified by the promise that it would help keep communism from pressing closer to America. In a similar manner, when the wages of the Negro laborers in Johannesburg, South Africa, were increased a few years ago, the mine-owners justified the increase because they believed it would keep the laborers from turning communistic. The scare of communism has been used to the limit in some churches to raise benevolence giving.

A missionary on leave from Rhodesia spoke to a New Jersey congregation and was introduced as a "fighter of communism."

What a judgment it is on the American church that a missionary must be known as a "fighter of communism" in order to solicit financial support! Apparently, our marching orders which read, "Go into all the world and preach the Gospel" are being replaced by, "Go and fight communism." A missionary secretary of a New Jersey presbytery commented to the author: "What would we do to raise money for missions if it were not for communism?" Her experience in speaking in various churches revealed that many Christians are on the defensive because they have forgotten the ringing orders which would enable them to be on the offensive.

Self-interest is constantly used as a motive in seeking support for secular benevolent work. A World War II poster read: "Give to China Relief—She is Fighting for You!" Or consider the slogan: "Give to the Cancer Fund, *you* may be next!" Or, "Be kind to *your* heart, give to the Heart Fund!" Many have been stirred to give to the Community Chest because, as the propaganda states, "It makes *your* community a better place in which to live." The motorist is reminded to drive safely: "Save a life; it might be *your own!*" Recently, the owner of a hotel also capitalized on the selfish motivation when he put signs in the rooms which read: "Don't smoke in bed; the ashes you spill may be your own."

In defense of this motivation it is pointed out that the strongest human drive is the drive for self-preservation, and it is only common sense to appeal to this drive. Nevertheless, the Christian faith declares there can be a drive in the human heart that is stronger than the drive for self-preservation, and this drive comes only through a new birth.

Missionary

With few exceptions the Christian church has been motivated to go into all the world because of her devotion to Jesus Christ.

There have been a few exceptions, and these have made the missionary program of the church open to attack at a very crucial point. When one casts his bread upon the waters, it sometimes returns many fold. Frequently, this has been the experience of missionary endeavors. However, in calling attention to these "returns" from missionary effort, the church has come dangerously close to making the "returns" the reasons for missions. The church may testify to the results of giving to missions; but, at the same time, care must be taken lest benevolence giving be recommended because of the material and temporal returns that might be enjoyed.

The Church of England was caught in this trap when it undertook a missionary project to the American Indians in the sixteenth century. As the following quotation shows, the appeal was based primarily on the value such an undertaking would be to England's commercial trade:

> Was, therefore, the scheme, here proposed, to be carried into execution, the Indian nations in America would soon be convinced, that their greatest temporal, as well as spiritual happiness, would be to cultivate peace and friendship with the English, and to become incorporated with them as one nation, under one government.
>
> It is easy to conceive, what an increased demand for European goods this would occasion. Should the spirit of cultivation take place among the Indians, the demand for utensils of every kind would be great indeed! If, therefore, 7,500 £ [pounds] a year, properly applied, would be a probable means of laying a foundation for propagating the gospel and introducing agriculture among them, what government upon earth would hesitate a moment to make the trial? [24]

This kind of propaganda has appeared in the present century at various times. *Current Literature* carried an article in December, 1906, contending a man should support the church financially "even if he be indifferent to the distinct evangelistic and religious work carried on." A New York clergyman, by the name of John Hutchinson, was quoted:

> One religious body put a million dollars into
> the Pacific Islands, Sixty per cent per annum has
> been paid on that investment. Statistics prove
> that every missionary to those islands has created
> an annual trade of fifty thousand dollars. . . . The
> industrial training which is so large and increas-
> ing a part of the education given to strange
> peoples, as well as to our homefolk, by mission-
> aries, ought to be applauded by any practical
> man.[25]

The article also quoted from the Canadian Government Blue Book for 1903, which observed: "As a Pagan the Indian was a liability, but as a Christian he becomes a national asset." In conclusion these words are added:

> More could well be said, but evidence enough
> has been piled up that the church in her effort
> to Christianize the pagans succeeds at least in
> adding tremendously to the world's wealth, and
> on this lowest possible ground she is to be re-
> garded as a good investment.

In 1910, a missionary rally was held in New York City, which received much publicity because of this emphasis on missions and foreign trade. One reporter noted that instead of hearing the "usual missionary talk," the audience heard a business emphasis from businessmen. "Naturally," he wrote, "it won their hearts, or rather, their pocketbooks." One of the speakers was George

Sherwood Eddy, who used motivating impulses, as follows, to stir his hearers:

> The Japanese government spent $50,000,000 recently in the United States solely because the Japanese engineers in charge of the work had been educated in the U.S. at the expense of the American missionaries, and had there imbibed Yankee notions which made it impossible for them to build a railroad along any other than American lines. Therefore, in one swoop, American commerce reaped a direct return of $50,000,000 from missionary effort.[26]

Another speaker at the same meeting, Arthur Judson Brown, attempted to convince his hearers that businessmen should support the foreign mission program because of the material returns. Reporting on one of his trips, he commented:

> In Korea I traveled in a car made in Delaware, drawn by a locomotive from Philadelphia over Pittsburgh rails, fastened by New York spikes to Oregon ties. I sat down to a meal that included Chicago beef, Pittsburgh pickles, and Minnesota flour. We could afford to support all the missionaries in Korea for the large and growing trade which they have developed with this country.[27]

The Saturday Evening Post, September, 1923, carried an article, entitled, "How Missionaries Help Foreign Trade," in which the author spoke of the "old and increasing debt" our commerce owes to the "patriotic missionary." Again, it was said that even those who were indifferent or actively hostile to the direct purpose of the missionary enterprise could "well afford to bear the cost of American missionary work in China for the sake of the large increase in trade which results from such efforts."

The president of "the largest mail-order house in the world" was quoted as follows:

> We have been outfitting missionaries as they started abroad and supplying them at their stations with most of the things they need for nearly half a century. We sent pianos to Africa, church bells to India, bicycles to China. First the missionary is our customer, and then his convert, his school pupils, and then other natives who see the things from America, and want some like them.[28]

The argument was pressed further by a quotation from a former collector of the port of San Francisco after he had returned from a trip to the Orient:

> Commercially speaking, the missionaries are the advance agents for American trade, and if businessmen only understood this matter, they would assist rather than discourage evangelical work in the East.[29]

Considerable publicity was received by Christian missions during World War II, because American boys saw the work of the missionary first hand. It was desirable for the American people to hear about missions, and Christians especially deserved to have these favorable reports. However, the danger of such publicity is that the church might try to move people to give to missions because of some lesser results of the missionary enterprise.

In Henry P. Van Dusen's book, *They Found the Church There*,[30] a number of cases are given of American boys who were "converted" to missions because they saw some of the practical results of missionary work. An Australian officer summarized the part played by the native Papuans:

> I doubt whether people realize how much we owe to these simple children of nature. Without their

aid, our position here would have quickly become
untenable, and perhaps the Japs would even now
have a stranglehold on our country.[31]

Numerous comments of this type were made by senators, officers, and privates. Their stories have been used to the limit in
some churches to get money for missions. The famous account
of the "Fuzzy-wuzzies," the natives of New Guinea who hid a
number of American fliers from the enemy and nursed them
back to health, was written up in a brochure and used by one
denomination as part of its 1949 promotional literature. The
cover carried a picture of the natives caring for the Americans,
then related the story, saying in effect, "Give to foreign missions
so when we get into another war, the natives will be on our
side." This is the danger—to take a secondary result of missions,
a result that is basically a dividend for the donor—and present
it as the main motive for future giving to missions.

Love

Professor Anders Nygren's book, *Eros and Agape*,[32] has
much to say about motives in the life of a Christian. He dis-
cusses two Greek words, both translated into English as "love."
The two words are the Greek *eros* and the Greek *agape*. *Eros*
is the upward movement of the human soul to seek the Divine.
Agape is God's own love, manifested in the life of his Son, who
came to seek and to save that which was lost. This love—*agape*
—is summed up in John 3:16 "For God so loved the world. . . ."
This love is a love with no strings attached! It expects nothing
in return!

The term "love" is used, of all places, in the game of tennis,
where "love" means zero or nothing. Thus, "fifteen-love" means
the score is fifteen to nothing. An understanding of the background of this terminology might help to clarify *agape* (love
that does not expect a return).

In the past, since the sixteenth century, men have entered contests and games to gain a maiden's hand, or a material prize. There were times, however, when a man entered a contest for no reason except for the joy of playing. Having no motive, except his love of the game, he entered for "love," or for "nothing." Consequently, the term "love" has come to mean zero in scoring tennis.

Another insight can be gained from the question put to God by Satan, concerning Job—"Does Job fear God for nought?" [33] That is, what is the motivation? What is the score? Is it for nothing—for love? Or, is there an ulterior motive behind Job's faithfulness?

God gave because he "so loved the world." There is no higher motive for Christian giving than to remember the grace of God in Jesus Christ. Can it be done? It can. Such giving has been demonstrated many times throughout the centuries of the Christian church, beginning with the church at Corinth. It was to that church the Apostle Paul wrote of the highest motive for giving—"For ye know the grace of our Lord Jesus Christ, that, though he was rich, yet for your sakes he became poor, that ye through his poverty might be rich," [34] consequently "every man according as he purposeth in his heart, so let him give; not grudgingly, or of necessity: for God loveth a cheerful giver." [35]

Is it an adequate motivation to give as a response to this grace? Is this enough to undergird our stewardship? It is enough. But enough only for those in whom Christ lives triumphantly, as only a Christian knows the grace of Jesus Christ.

XII

Guiding Principles

Living in the cash-and-credit economy of the present day, we need to be disciplined by principles or guides in order to meet the multiple financial demands which life places upon us. A budget of some kind is necessary, and certain items in the budget must be given priority. Unless an individual has unlimited financial means, he must administer his financial matters according to some plan. Otherwise, he will be in trouble with his creditors, or without the means to buy the necessities of life.

Likewise, if one is to learn the art of Christian giving and be a faithful steward of God, there are certain principles he must observe in his stewardship. This chapter attempts, first, to show the groundwork which has been laid by the Stewardship Movement of the past one hundred years, and, second, to set forth the two basic principles of Christian giving which have the authority of both Scripture and logic.

Stewardship

The words "steward" and "stewardship" appear in Scripture a number of times, but are used in different ways. First, the title "steward" is given to one who has the responsibility of overseer, manager, foreman, or administrator, and he is directly responsible to the head of the household. The property of which he is in charge is not his; it belongs to his lord. The word "stew-

ard" is used, in this sense, in the Old and the New Testament.[1]
It was this interpretation which gave content to the stewardship
movement of the middle part of the nineteenth century.

The second meaning which Scripture gives to the term "steward" is found in such passages as I Corinthians 4:1, Titus 1:7,
and I Peter 4:10. Here the Christian is admonished to be a faithful steward of "the mysteries of God," and of "the manifold
Grace of God." This meaning has not had a very prominent
place in stewardship during the past hundred and fifty years,
and it may be that the stewardship movement has lacked
strength and revolutionary power because of this fact. It is
true that God is owner of all and we are stewards, but such a
statement can be made by non-Christians; it is not specifically
an evangelical statement. However, when a Christian realizes he
is a steward of God's gift to the world, he sees that faithfulness
in his stewardship will determine the extent to which he carries
the gospel into all the world. In a cash-and-credit economy one's
stewardship of the "mysteries of God" is measured, in part, by
his stewardship of material possessions.

The Stewardship Movement. It would be a case of blind pro-
vincialism to discuss stewardship as though it were a movement
identified with—or characteristic of—American churches. Also,
it would be presumptuous to imply that the principles of stewardship are products of the nineteenth and twentieth centuries.
But there has been a definite movement of Christian stewardship
in the last century, and the churches of America have shared in
the movement.

Toward the close of the eighteenth century and early in the
nineteenth century, an important awakening helped to prepare
the way for the stewardship movement that was soon to follow.
It began when the churches of America began to catch a new
vision of home and foreign missions and formed societies with
missionary purposes as their goals. Numerous missionary socie-

ties were formed in nearly all denominations from 1798 through 1826.

Then, the decade between 1840 and 1850 saw an arousing of American Christians to a new concern for humanity throughout the world, caused by the European revolutions and an unprecedented trend toward democratic governments. Tract societies—on both sides of the Atlantic—encouraged thinking on the relation between a man, his property, and his God, by conducting contests for the best essays on the subject of stewardship. The first three prizes in the contest sponsored by the Methodist Episcopal Church were awarded to essays entitled, "The Great Reform," "The Great Question," and "Property Consecrated." [2] The Presbyterian, Congregational, and Baptist Churches in America co-operated with the American Tract Society to promote a contest similar to that of the Methodists. It attracted 175 manuscripts, with the leading essays being "The Faithful Steward," [3] "The Divine Law of Beneficence," [4] and "The Good Steward." [5]

A group of Evangelicals in the north of Ireland conducted a contest, too, known as the "Ulster Prizes," and published the five leading essays in one book under the title *Gold and the Gospel*,[6] which sold 30,000 copies!

The dark days of the Civil War (1861-1862) undoubtedly crippled the stewardship movement. In the years following the war, books and essays on stewardship continued to be published, but the vision of the people was not equal to the increased wealth enjoyed by the nation by the year 1880. Nevertheless, the stewardship theme was kept alive, and early in the twentieth century a lay movement—The Laymen's Missionary Movement —was launched and missions given a new impetus through increased giving.

The Laymen's Movement is a "revival of religion in the very truest sense of the word. There is no wild excitement with regard to it, and it is supremely unselfish in its purpose and aims." [7] By enlisting mature men—leading businessmen who previously had been uninterested in the church—the movement helped to put the entire church upon a better financial basis. Emphasis was placed, first, upon the stewardship of life, which manifested itself in larger gifts to the church.

Two common fallacies exist in our stewardship thinking, and both must be corrected. First, we seem to have had the idea that we can expect good fruit from a corrupt tree. That is, we have conducted the administration and finances of the church as though non-Christians could exemplify evangelical steward-ship. Yet, anyone who has ministered to a congregation soon has discovered that few things are more frustrating than trying to inspire a non-Christian to give as though he were a Christian. We shall need to face up to the possibility that our spirituality may have to be increased before we can expect more generous giving. Miles Taber has written:

> We have not reached the saturation point in
> what we ought to give, but I believe we have about
> reached the saturation point in what we will give
> in our present spiritual state. It would seem
> then, that the remedy is not more begging and
> pleading, or new schemes for raising money. What
> we need is an experience with God that results
> in the reign of the Holy Spirit in all our lives. [8]

A second fallacy in stewardship thinking is the idea that a man automatically exemplifies evangelical stewardship simply by accepting Christ as his Lord and Savior. This fallacy arises because we have failed to recognize that the many implications of the gospel are not immediately clear. The Christian faith has implications for all areas of life, but sometimes these implica-tions are hidden and must be brought out into the open as one grows in faith. Hence, if Christians are to learn to express their faith in generous giving, they must be given certain guiding principles.

The remainder of this chapter is devoted to the two basic principles of giving which are biblically and logically sound. Both are necessary if the average person is to learn the art of Christian giving. The first principle calls for giving according to one's ability to give, a principle which we shall call "proportionate giving." The second basic principle is the recognition that Christ comes first in all things. As a manifestation of the place that Christ has in one's life, the Christian will set aside the Lord's portion first. This principle will be called "first-fruit giving."

Proportionate Giving

To understand the meaning of proportionate giving, one must see a significant difference between dedicating oneself to a certain proportion and merely giving an arbitrary amount in dollars and cents. Obviously, no matter what one gives, it will be a proportion of his income—but the term proportionate giving implies that the individual is guided in his giving according to a *specific* proportion which he has designated.

A simple test, which one might take to determine the nature of his giving, would be to ask, "Have I set aside, earmarked, or dedicated a specific proportion of my income for the work of Christ? . . . Or, is my giving merely an arbitrary amount which the immediate factors at hand determine?" Of course, whenever a need presents itself, one must decide the particular amount he is going to give to that specific cause. But the distinguishing question remains: is the amount to be drawn from a predetermined or earmarked percentage of income? . . . or, is the amount to be decided by what can be afforded at the moment? If one has decided on a specific proportion—previous to the time the giving begins—he is practicing proportionate giving. If, on the other hand, one merely gives an arbitrary amount, be it large or small, and has no idea as to what proportion his giving is until it is figured at the end of the year, he is not practicing proportionate giving.

This differentiation is vital at two points. First, in proportionate giving, one makes provision for Christ's work regardless of other claims that may be made upon one's personal or family budget during the year. On the other hand, when one waits until a need presents itself and then reaches into his pocket to see what he can spare, he makes the work of Christ compete with all the other unforeseen demands which might arise.

Second, proportionate giving offers equal standing to all people regardless of their material possessions. Regardless of the emphasis which man may place upon the size of a gift in dollars and cents, the fact remains that God sees every gift in relation to income or ability to give.

The principle of proportionate giving is set forth in the Old and New Testament. It underlies the Old Testament teaching on tithing, since tithing is always proportionate giving. In the New Testament, our Lord and Paul expound the principle of proportionate giving. Jesus taught that a man's giving of himself or of his talents was to be governed according to what he possessed. The parable of the talents, and the poor widow's mite are cases in point. Paul, likewise, taught proportionate giving when he urged the people to lay by in store upon the first day of the week as God has prospered them.

In our day, some churches attempt to distribute, equally, the financial responsibility of the church among the members, talking about average gifts, or by dividing the total amount of the budget by the number of members and arriving at a suggested gift. Such practices are dangerous as they detract from proportionate giving, based upon one's ability to give.

So important is this matter of proportionate giving that some church bodies are encouraging people merely to indicate on the pledge card the percentage they will give; the amount in dollars and cents is not recorded. The one objection to this, on the part of some persons, is that it reveals the income of the members. In any event, this emphasis is true to the first basic principle of Christian stewardship—proportionate giving.

First Fruits

Either God has first place in the life of a man or he has no place. There is no middle ground. By setting aside or earmarking God's portion *first*—and the stress is on *first*—the Christian manifests through his economic life the place God has in his entire life. To do so is first-fruits giving.

First fruits were given long before the Christian era; they were encouraged, also, in the Christian church from its beginning. The significant thing about first fruits was the principle, not the amount. Tradition sometimes has specified certain amounts as a guide in first-fruits giving, but whenever such an attempt is made, the spirit or principle of first fruits is destroyed. First-fruits giving is not concerned with the amount of the gift; rather, it is concerned that God's portion, whatever it may be, is to be set aside *first*.

If a man is going to do this gladly, he will have to give himself completely to Christ, first. In this surrender, he will come to believe God's kingdom to be the most important thing in the world. Christ will come first in his whole life and he will put Christ first in all things, even in the budget.

Perhaps it is in order to raise the question as to what the record has been in this respect. Does the record show that Christians have exemplified first-fruits giving? It does not! The facts reveal that neither congregations nor individuals have manifested the spirit of first-fruits giving.

For instance, a study of the per-capita giving of the denominations reporting annually to the Department of Stewardship and

Benevolence of the National Council of the Churches of Christ in the U.S.A. shows that congregations have been inclined to care for their own needs before allowing for others' needs.

In 1920 the benevolent giving of churches averaged 26.7 per cent of the total giving, and in 1921 the average was 30.8 per cent. However, from 1922 to 1946 the percentage given to benevolences decreases until it reaches a low of 12.2 per cent. Since 1947 the percentage has shown a general increase; however, as late as 1958 and 1959 the benevolence giving of 35 denominations averaged only 18.5 per cent of the total giving. This hardly represents first-fruits giving!

Note that in 1920 the benevolent giving of churches averaged 26.7 per cent of the total giving, but it averaged only 17.7 per cent in 1930 and only 13.4 per cent in 1940. Note, too, the average per cent given to benevolence in 1941—12.8 per cent as compared to 13.3 per cent in 1951 (less than half the percentage given in 1921!).

Another indication of a lack of faithfulness to the principle of first-fruits giving can be seen in the way congregations have supported their ministers. Whether we like it or not, the support of the ministry can be identified with giving to God. As long as we have an ecclesiastical organization which calls for a paid clergy, supporting the minister, virtually, is giving to God.

For years ministers have been considered parasites on the community, or a liability to be endured. Appeals have been made, as far back as 1836, to congregations to cease referring to their ministers as "beggars." [9]

An essay written in 1866, "The Muzzled Ox," attempted to state a case for the paid ministry. The author was led to write the essay because it could ". . . scarcely be questioned that there are a large number of faithful and laborious Ministers in our land who receive but a very inadequate pecuniary support." [10]

Fifty years ago, the son of a minister wrote a story about his father who died and left "a good name and a butcher's bill," [11] indicating that he, too, was entering the ministry, but could not pay the cost of his education out of his meager salary. The periodical carrying the story asked the readers if this was an exceptional case. Sixteen answers were published in a later issue. One writer thought the young minister was a poor businessman! Another felt he lacked faith, saying, "The Lord will provide." And a third, an elder in the Presbyterian Church, thought the young man's case was exceptional. The remaining thirteen, however, gave stories of hardship similar to that of the young man. [12]

At that time, the reports of the Census Bureau (1913) indicated the average annual salaries of ministers outside the large cities were as follows:

Southern Baptist Convention (White) . . . $	334
Disciples	526
United Brethren	547
Methodist Episcopal (South)	681
Northern Baptist Convention (White) . . .	683
Presbyterian Church in U.S. (South)	857
Congregational	880
Reformed Church in America	923
Presbyterian Church in U.S.A. (North) . .	977
Methodist Episcopal (North)	743
Lutheran	744
Universalist	987
Protestant Episcopal	994
Unitarian	1,221

The salary situation, apparently, was no better by 1919; for, in that year, *The Literary Digest* printed a cartoon depicting preachers on strike for higher salaries, showing the distinguished gentlemen carrying signs which read: "Even the worm finally turns" . . . "We will no longer starve while we save your souls from hell" . . . "A new dress for the wife" . . . "We demand a full dinner pail" . . . "Remember our kiddies." A rather ironic

suggestion was made that the preachers should form an organization, "The Amalgamated Association for the Protection and
Promotion of Progressive Preachers." [13]

The plight of the minister in 1923 was summarized in an
article "From Preaching to Plastering"; "He spread the Gospel
until he was tired and hungry. Then he left the pulpit and
spread plaster—at $500 a month!" [14] This same account cited
an investigation made by *The Homiletic Review*. The results are
itemized in the following table:

Table II

AVERAGE WEEKLY SALARY OF MINISTERS OF SIX DENOMINATIONS
COMPARED WITH AVERAGE WEEKLY SALARY OF OTHER WORKERS
ACCORDING TO AN INVESTIGATION CONDUCTED IN 1923

Denomination	Average Weekly Salary
Evangelical Synod	$17.30
Baptist, North	25.00
Methodist Episcopal, South	28.65
Methodist Episcopal, North	29.44
Presbyterian, South	28.58
Presbyterian, North	34.60

Type of Worker	Average Weekly Salary
Boot and shoe worker	$25.04
Furniture maker	28.63
Auto maker	30.47
Foundryman	31.51
Electrical worker	31.86
Iron and steel worker	37.81
Hodcarrier	30.14
Cement finisher	41.27
Mason	51.57
Plumber	47.17
Plasterer	55.79
Bricklayer	55.92

Generally, ministers have suffered financial hardships, not because of the poverty of the people, but because the people have tried to support the church with what has been left after all other bills have been paid. First-fruits giving has been unknown to most Christians.

A telling comparison of values was printed by *The Literary Digest,* February 16, 1924, when a "weary pastor" recorded items he gleaned from the local newspaper along with gleanings from his church records. Here are a few of the "deadly" comparisons:

NEWS ITEMS	CHURCH RECORDS
Mrs. A. entertained eight intimate friends with a dinner yesterday at the ———, after which she took the party to the Majestic Theater to see ———.	Mrs. A. contributes $3.60 a year to the missionary societies of her church. She has been a *deeply* interested member of these organizations for 18 years.
Mr. and Mrs. B. left last night for New York, where they will attend the World Series. They will be gone about three weeks, during which time they will visit Niagara and other points of interest in that section.	Mr. B. sent his check to the treasurer for $60, covering his annual contribution for the support of the church and benevolences, accompanying it with a note saying he was sorry it had to be less than last year.
Mr. E. and family arrived at church last Sunday in their new Lincoln sedan, which he recently purchased preparatory to a Western tour of six weeks, upon which they leave next Sunday.	Mr. E. pays his $40 regularly each year the week before Conference, but raises serious objection to the extravagance with which the people's money is spent by our mission workers.
Among the 300 guests at the Governor's reception, no one was more elegantly attired than Mrs. G. Her rare jewels added to her	Mrs. G. found it impossible to comply with the suggestion of the committee that she increase her support to the church by 25¢

native charm. Mrs. G., accompanied by her two daughters,
will leave in a few days for a
four months' European trip.

a week on account of increased
cost of coal and labor. She would
pay just as she had been doing,
thirty-five cents a week.

The following story makes the same point: namely, the Lord
usually gets what is left over. A little boy had been given two
nickels one Sunday morning; one was to be his Sunday School
offering, the other was his to spend at the candy store. On his
way to Sunday School—as he was flipping one nickel in the air
—one nickel fell through his fingers, rolled into the gutter drain
out of sight. "Well, I'm sorry, Lord," he mused, "but there goes
your nickel." So it has been with the Christian and his money.

It need not be that way, however; for, when once a Christian
accepts, as valid, proportionate giving and first-fruits giving,
then he asks: what is the Lord's proportion to be? Some Christians answer this question quite simply, saying, "a tithe." Others
have rejected tithing as a worthy standard of giving. In the following chapter, an attempt is made to evaluate the place of
tithing as a schoolmaster or as a self-discipline in Christian
giving.

XIII

The Discipline
of Tithing

Tithing is one of the most controversial financial issues in the church today. This controversy rages within the individual denominations as well as between and among them. On the one hand, there are those who uphold tithing as an integral part of the Christian life, believing it is required of every Christian. At the other extreme, there are those who reject tithing as a Christian practice along with circumcision, foot washing, and the observance of the dietary laws. Between these two extremes are many variations of interpretations and opinions.

A Rise in Interest

Previous to the mid-1880's little attention was given to tithing in the American churches. This was due to a natural reaction against the enforced system of tithing in England and on the Continent. The few attempts to institute tithing in the early American churches were weak, and they met with general hostility. Also, the missionary vision of the churches prior to the nineteenth century was lacking, enabling subscription lists, pew rents, and lotteries to meet the financial needs of the rather limited local program.

Happily, the past one hundred years have witnessed a renewed interest in tithing. In fact, the growing interest since the middle of the nineteenth century has culminated in what could be called a tithing movement today. Currently, the promotional literature in many denominations makes a strong emphasis on tithing.

The roots of this development go back to the first thirty years of the nineteenth century, when at least twenty missionary societies were organized by churches in the United States. An interest in missions always creates an interest in giving. In this case it led to various stewardship movements among the laity. Then, too, a reaction against liberal theology and higher criticism led to a strict literalism, which accepted the Old Testament as equal in authority with the New Testament and concluded that tithing was God's method of financing the church.

Another factor causing a rise in an interest in tithing was a growing dissatisfaction with many of the methods by which the church was being financed. The pew-rent system was under critical attack, because it had emphasized social distinctions and militated against evangelism. The church was a bit ashamed of the fact that the public conscience against lotteries had been aroused before the conscience of the church. Church suppers, bazaars, and sales were dominating the efforts of the people to such an extent that little time was left for the spiritual program of the church. Ministers' salaries were low and in arrears, and they were forced to undergo a periodical "pounding" or "donation party."

These and other questionable methods of financing the church led ministers to ask what God's plan was for his church. Many believed tithing was the cure-all for problems in church finance.

Finally, there is no question that the Laymen's Movement, led by Thomas Kane, had a significant influence in stirring new interest in tithing. As indicated in a previous chapter, Kane, a presbyterian elder, first discovered tithing for himself and then set out to introduce others to it, circulating pamphlets on tithing at his own expense, under the name of "Layman."

The motives for tithing, expressed in the literature of this period, were varied. Some writers drew their authority from the fact of universality. Henry Lansdell, for example, explored extensively the practices of tithing among many nations, giving evidence of tithing among Egyptians, Babylonians, Persians, Phoenicians, Arabians, Greeks, and Romans.[1]

Probably the most common source of authority of the writers of this period was the Old Testament, particularly the third chapter of Malachi, where the prophet asks, "Would a man rob God?" The promises assured by the prophet were often quoted.

An impressive number of personal testimonies concerning the material blessings that come from tithing, plus scriptural passages that promise prosperity, have also become authority for tithing.

Harvey Reeves Calkins urged tithing to be practiced as an acknowledgment of God's ownership and man's stewardship. In his book, *A Man and His Money*,[2] he stressed the tithe as an act of acknowledgment and the use of the remaining nine-tenths as a witness to stewardship. The book, published in 1914, continues to influence churchmen to this day.

Throughout its development in contemporary Christian thought, tithing has met with a good deal of opposition. Some churchmen reject it as a standard of giving because they believe it has dangers. To wit—the man who feels slightly uncomfortable in the acquisition of wealth by questionable means may find a salve for his conscience by giving the Lord a tithe. One thoughtful opponent wrote: "Any teaching of the church which tends to ethicize what is essentially unethical must finally be detrimental to the task of making civilization itself ethical." [3] Continuing, he believes all power or privilege is unethical unless all of it is shared. He draws the case of a man with an income of $100,000 a year, who, being a tither, gives $10,000 each year for religious and benevolent purposes. Yet, he still has $90,000 to spend on himself. Thus, the $10,000 gift, which might serve to quiet a conscience, can obscure the essentially unethical nature of this man's relationship to his brother.

In answer to this, the advocates of tithing, such as Mr. Calkins, would say the man who gives only a tenth of $100,000 may be faithful in acknowledging his partnership with God, but by keeping $90,000 for himself, he fails to be a true steward.

A very thoughtful objection to tithing comes from a group of biblical scholars who believe the Old Testament passages on tithing have been misinterpreted. They assert that the Old Testament presents a fusion of many ritual or ceremonial offerings and fees, originating in many ways, formally carrying various local names, and that the technical term "tithe" has come to be applied to them. Further, they claim the biblical term "tithe" or "tenth" merely meant a fraction, portion, or percentage. A. H. Godbey observes that many ancient peoples could count only to ten, or less; hence, to indicate a *portion,* it is possible that the convenient proportion of a tenth was used. Godbey is certain that primitive people gave first fruits or harvest offerings, but he seriously doubts that these first fruits or tithes were measured out to equal a tenth.[4]

J. M. Powis Smith and other scholars maintain that the Deuteronomic law applied the name "tithe" to the offering of the first fruits.[5] His conviction is strengthened by a number of factors. First, the community was expected to take its tithe to Jerusalem and eat it all—as well as the firstlings of flocks and herds—at a single feast. For this to be possible, the crops would have had to be quite small. If the people could eat one-tenth of the year's produce at a single feast, how could they subsist for the remainder of the year on the remaining nine-tenths? The only probable answer, according to Smith, is that the tithe was not a full tenth.

A second fact which causes some doubt as to the exact proportion of the "tithe" is found in I Samuel 8:15,17. The king demanded a tithe of the flocks and the produce of the fields; but, according to I Kings 4:7,22, the land was organized into twelve districts, each of which was responsible for a month's support of the royal establishment. This could mean the poor farmer was taxed at least twice, totaling one-fifth or more of all he raised. Though this is not impossible, Smith believes it improbable in light of the Deuteronomic law's benevolent attitude toward the poor. Again, he concludes the tithe did not represent a full tenth.

A third complication is seen in the institution of the fallow year. It involved an average annual loss to the farmer and the country of one-seventh of the products of the soil. The charity tithe of the third year also raises questions. This tithe (Deuteronomy 14:28 and 26:12) prescribes that "all the tithe of that increase in that year" shall be brought forth and deposited within the gates as a source of supply for the hungry Levites, sojourners, fatherless, and widows of the town. If, in the references above, tithes actually represented one-tenth, the Hebrew farmer gave between a fourth and a third of his income—in addition to other taxations and rents.

Perhaps the most serious objection to tithing is the fact it might be interpreted in such a way as to do damage to the evangelical message. This error might express itself in a number of ways. For instance, one pastor insists that it encourages a type of self-righteousness, saying, "I don't have a tither in my church who is not a Pharisee."

A wrong interpretation of tithing could also give rise to the idea of keeping the law for the sake of merit. And this cannot be glossed over, since one of the most persistent heresies in the Christian church has been the notion that man attains salvation by keeping the law or by performing acceptable acts. The message of nonevangelical religions centers in what man can do to reach God; but evangelical Christianity is a message of what God has done for man. Thus, it is crucial that tithing, as a discipline, be presented only to those who are in Christ. It must be presented from this side of the Cross.

Tithing Defined

What is tithing? If we are to communicate intelligently, we must define our terms. Basically, *tithing is the practice of giving a tenth of one's income.* For a Christian, however, certain additions become necessary. To this "core" definition must be added, first, the object of the gift. Second, the motivation is a part of the definition. Third, if we are to carry out Paul's instructions to be systematic, our definition will speak of regularity. And, finally, to stress the voluntary principle, we shall include something about self-discipline.

Accordingly, a possible definition of Christian tithing might be as follows: *Christian tithing is the self-discipline of setting aside regularly for Christ's work a tithe of one's income as an acknowledgment of God's ownership of all things, including man himself, and as a response to God's love as revealed in Jesus Christ.*

Even if this definition is acceptable, it cannot be clear until one defines some of the terms within the definition. At least, four terms or phrases need clarification—"tithe," "income," "work of Christ," and "acknowledgment."

A "tithe" is 10 per cent. By giving a tithe, one obviously gives proportionately, the proportion being 10 per cent. But not all proportionate giving is tithing. One might give .001 per cent of his income and still be giving on a proportionate basis; but, to tithe, it is necessary to understand the proportion to be 10 per cent.

This definition is being stressed because some folks have made tithing and proportionate giving synonymous. In some churches, tithing is presented with the suggestion that the tithe be at least 5 per cent. That is not tithing. It is impossible to be intellectually honest and call such proportionate giving by the name of "tithing." This may sound very legalistic; however, it is an attempt to be honest in the use of terminology.

To communicate satisfactorily, the word "income" must be understood, too. Usually, the word income is preceded by one of two adjectives "gross" or "net." "Gross" refers to the whole or entire income, while "net" designates that which is clear again or profit. In the definition of tithing, presented here, "income" means "net income." The income tax regulations suggest a rather fair basis on which to arrive at one's "net" income, namely, gross income less business or professional expenses.

The question is raised frequently as to whether one's income tax is to be deducted before figuring one's tithe. If we are going to be consistent in our definition, we must allow income tax to be deducted before one figures his proportionate gift, whether it be a tenth or some other proportion. The present income tax system actually creates a lien against a man's income. It is an absolute tax and is in the same category as a necessary expense. Actually, the amount of the tax cannot be considered income if one is to figure his "increase" or profit on a realistic basis.

We need, also, to recognize that income tax is subject to change; and, if our principle of tithing is sound, it must be so defined as to remain valid regardless of changes in taxation. To illustrate, suppose a government writes a tax law which imposes a tax in excess of 90 per cent of one's income. In such a case, a man who set aside his tithe before taxation would be giving more than he actually had—mathematically, it would be impossible to tithe.

This discussion may seem absurd, but it points out the fallacy of establishing any kind of proportionate giving on any other basis than one's "net" increase. The tithe merely establishes a base, and the one who learns this discipline in a Christian spirit will move beyond 10 per cent.

Reference is made in our definition to the "work of Christ." The concern, at this point, is whether the entire tithe should be given to the church, or whether there are humanitarian causes independent of the church worthy of part of the tithe. Some people believe the entire tithe should be appropriated to the church, quoting Malachi 3:10, "Bring ye all the tithe into the storehouse. . . ." Others believe the Christian steward has the responsibility of appropriating his gifts. Probably, the greater part of the Christian's giving will be administered through the channels of the church. It is, however, the individual's responsibility to share in other programs which are expressions of the spirit of Christ.

This position is based, in part, on the conviction that some agencies and movements have been created independent of the church because the church has been neglectful. In any event, each individual must arrive at a philosophy on all these matters, a philosophy he believes to be consistent with his evangelical faith and commitment.

The significance of the term "acknowledgment" can be seen when this question is posed: is a tenth intended to be the minimum gift or a maximum gift? Some notable writers have emphasized the giving of a tenth as an acknowledgment of God's ownership, and anything above the tenth is a matter of one's faithfulness in his stewardship. It must be remembered that we are to be faithful stewards of all that we have, and though the tenth may be an acknowledgment that all belongs to God, we are still under the discipline of Christian stewards in what we do with the remaining nine-tenths.

Tithers usually use the figure of 10 per cent as a minimum or base, moving to higher percentages of giving once they have lived with the discipline. There seems to be a "giving barrier" similar to the "sound barrier," which is encountered by the high-speed planes. Up to a certain speed—the speed of sound—the air in front of a plane creates a "drag" that increases with the increased speed of the plane. But once the speed of the plane exceeds the speed of sound, the craft moves on with an unprecedented freedom to greater and greater speeds. In a similar sense, tithing seems to break the "barrier" to liberal giving. This is not to say the figure of 10 per cent is magical, or is as consistent as the laws of speed and sound. Nevertheless, the growing testimony of tithers seems to be that once the discipline of tithing is established—as a reasonable first step in giving—a person finds increased ease and joy in additional giving.

Five Witnesses for Tithing

Is there a case for tithing? Someone has claimed that the more arguments one presents for a cause, the weaker the case becomes. It also has been observed that one strong argument is better than a dozen weak arguments. Whatever the case may be, five witnesses are presented here for tithing.

The Witness of the Scriptures. Proof texts cannot be used to find the Old Testament message on tithing for Christians. Instead, it becomes necessary to determine the motives for the Hebrew's tithe. Passages in the Old Testament support three motives for tithing.

First, there are passages in which tithing appears to be legalistic transactions, either to satisfy the stern demands of God or to bargain with God for material blessings. Second, a very practical motive for tithing is given—to provide support for the Levites. Finally, a motivation which runs through much of the tithing emphasis is that of gratitude to God, an acknowledgment of his ownership of all.

Primarily, the motivation for the Christian is the third one; it has become a principle of religious devotion, an expression of gratitude, and an acknowledgment of God as creator and man as creature.

As we turn to the New Testament witness for tithing, the words of our Lord are most important. Did Jesus urge tithing? He mentioned it only twice. Once, in speaking of the Pharisees, he said the man with a repentant spirit went away justified, not the man who boasted of his tithing and other good deeds. Tithing is neither endorsed nor condemned. In Christ's other reference to tithing (Matthew 23:23) he commented, ". . . these ye ought to have done, and not to leave the other undone." Writing in *The Interpreter's Bible,* Sherman E. Johnson charges this phrase with spoiling the point of the saying, indicating it may have been added by Matthew.[6] Johnson adds, however, that Jesus certainly would have insisted the tithe law of Deuteronomy must be kept, but not the Pharisaic elaborations. Consequently, it can be concluded that our Lord commended tithing.

In a sense, the Apostle Paul was close to the point of recommending tithing; in another sense, he was far from it. His instructions to the Corinthians, urging them to set aside, systematically, a proportion of their income comes close to suggesting tithing. Conjecture leads one to believe he avoided the mention of it because of his fear that legalism might defeat the gospel.

The theme of the Epistle to the Hebrews is that God, who spoke in the past by the prophets, has in these last days spoken unto us by his son; and, after the order of Melchizedec, Jesus is our high priest who has acted once and for all. There is a subtle suggestion in this book. In the first place, the Old Testament allows for a paid priesthood, providing for the support of that priesthood by the tithe. Likewise, the New Testament allows for a paid clergy, without specific provisions for financing the clergy. From a practical standpoint, if tithes were in order for the support of a priesthood who had to go daily to make sacrifices, surely they are justified to make known the saving power of that high priest who once for all gave himself as a sacrifice for the sins of the world, even Jesus Christ.

The Witness of Need. The voice of need shouts loudly in behalf of tithing as a Christian discipline. Among many there is doubt whether the task before the church today can be done with less than a tithe from its members. It is possible that the task demands far more than a mere tithe. We cannot spend billions of dollars for war and pennies for Christ, and expect the kingdom of God to come and the will of God to be done on earth!

The effectiveness of the church in our day is subject to financial support, and the evangelistic program of the Body of Christ depends upon money. And the sad testimony of the contemporary church is that her program has been limited critically, because financial support has not been adequate.

When the Japanese attacked Pearl Harbor, many church members became cynical, saying, "They turn on us, after all the money we sent to them through missions." Did we send them a lot of money through missions? Not according to one churchman who pointed out that the total amount of money given to Japan by all denominations within the period of Christian missionary work in Japan would not buy two of the battleships that were sunk in the bay at Pearl Harbor!

A secretary of missions of one denominational board had to turn a young couple away from China for lack of sufficient funds on the same day that a friend—an executive of an oil company —offered a tremendous salary to another young couple, if they would go to work for the oil company in South America. That is a parable. We cannot spend billions of dollars for industry in other countries and pennies for missions, and expect the Church of Jesus Christ to make much of an impact!

The average per capita gift to Foreign Missions of thirty-five denominations reporting in 1959 was $2.26—less than one cent per member per day; in fact, less than five cents per member per week.

After twenty centuries, the Christian people have not manifested sufficient stewardship to carry out the Lord's commission: "Go into all the world and preach the gospel." If Christians were to adopt the self-discipline of tithing, there would be meat in the Lord's house.

The Witness of Tithing Churches. Tithing is upheld as a minimum standard of giving by some denominations in Protestantism today. Some of the other denominations have criticized their theology, calling their tithing "legalistic." However, it is not always clear where self-discipline leaves off and legalism begins.

A look at the per-capita giving of some of these denominations is enlightening. The following table is based on the 1959 statistical report (published November 1, 1960) of the Department of Stewardship and Benevolence of the National Council of the Churches of Christ in the U.S.A. The first ten denominations place a strong emphasis upon tithing. The denominations in the second group of ten generally encourage tithing, but they do not make this discipline a major emphasis.

Group One	*Per Capita Gift*
Pentecostal Holiness	$113.30
United Brethren	119.69
Church of the Nazarene	135.51
Orthodox Presbyterian	161.17
Evangelical Covenant	164.82
Brethren in Christ	168.31
Pilgrim Holiness	200.48
Evangelical Free Church	203.54
Wesleyan Methodist	228.13
Free Methodist	269.71

Group Two

Baptist, American Convention	$ 48.52
Methodist	52.18
Christian (Disciples of Christ)	60.93
Protestant Episcopal	61.36
United Lutheran	68.29
Congregational Christian	71.12
American Lutheran	73.52
Evangelical and Reformed	80.92
United Presbyterian, U.S.A.	82.30
Missouri Synod Lutheran	93.89

A comparison of per-capita giving to foreign missions is even more startling. In 1959 the Methodists gave an average of $1.13. The United Presbyterians gave an average of $2.98. The American Baptist Convention showed an average of $1.44, as did the Protestant Episcopal. However, the per-capita giving to foreign missions of the denominations who stress tithing is much higher. The Pilgrim Holiness show an average of $14.57; the Brethren in Christ, $15.75; the Orthodox Presbyterian, $17.39; the Seventh Day Adventists, $31.98; and the Evangelical Free Church, $36.64.

There are some hidden factors in these figures. For example, it is pointed out, frequently, that the Seventh Day Adventists collect money from people of other denominations and credit it to their total receipts. Though this may be true, it is also possible that other denominations collect a good bit from people not members of their communions through merchandising and other means.

A relationship exists between the size of the denomination and the efficiency of its giving. As a denomination becomes larger, it becomes more difficult to reach all the members with a program of stewardship. Furthermore, the denomination reaching into lower-income areas of the nation cannot expect to show as high a per capita as a denomination concentrating its ministry among higher-income people. In spite of these factors, the tithing churches have left the rest far behind in giving.

The witness of a small church in Tulsa, Oklahoma, The John Knox Presbyterian Church, testifies to the increased giving that results when a few members accept the challenge to tithe. With 101 families pledging, the total pledges increased from $13,837 in 1951 to $25,829 in 1952. The number of tithers increased from 16 to 36. In 1951, for example, 9 persons or families made an average pledge of $4.44 per week, a total of $2,077.92 for the year. In 1952 those same persons made an average pledge of $11.44 per week, a total of $5,353.92.[7]

The witness stands—tithing churches give far more generously than nontithing churches, for the simple reason that tithers are much more generous than nontithers. "By their fruits ye shall know them."

The Witness of Individual Tithers. This witness wishes to speak to the fact that tithers like to tithe. Tithing has been tested thousands of times in the laboratory of human experience. What is the verdict? It may be stated in several ways; however, with very few exceptions, people who have tried tithing, heartily recommend it to others, and they, themselves, have no desire to give it up.

The man who advocates tithing is the man who has given it a fair try in his life; the man who rejects it is the man who has not given it a fair try. Exceptions to this statement are few. The author has interviewed hundreds of people concerning their giving, and in only two cases found people who tried tithing and then gave it up, to return to a former practice of unplanned giving. In one of these cases, a man tithed during his Army life, but discontinued it after he was discharged. In the other case, a man tried tithing because someone assured him his business would turn out better if he tithed. He concluded, "Tithing doesn't work," since his business was no better after the first six months of tithing.

People begin tithing for many reasons, some of them questionable—but, after being released from their narrow conceptions, they continue to tithe. Tithers enjoy tithing. Why?

Basically, people enjoy tithing because it carries its own reward. To the tither, it is a natural thing to do. It fits into religious life like prayer, public worship, and personal witness. It is natural—that is, it is an integral part of man's Christian life. When one does natural things he expects certain things to happen. To wit—in eating one is satisfied; it has its own rewards; to live is to "enjoy" breathing; in sleeping one awakens refreshed; in tithing the tither enjoys tithing. After one practices it for awhile, he believes it would be unnatural to give it up.

Things in life have to be experienced to be understood or appreciated. Being a Christian is like that. Tithing is like that, too —consequently, "taste and see."

The Witness of Men's Need of Discipline. The late Peter Marshall, in defending the stand he had taken in regard to social drinking, said to a dinner friend: "I heard somebody say the other day that the future of our world is going to be in the hands of disciplined people. That's true." If the Christian church is to fulfill her appointed task, Christians must accept certain disciplines.

In recent years, Protestantism has experienced a revived interest in Christian discipline. The Methodists have been calling these disciplines "Holy Habits." Whatever they may be called, disciplines are necessary if the individual Christian is to experience the fullness of his faith and if the church is to fulfill her mission.

These disciplines are prayer, Scripture reading, public worship, tithing. Today, it takes discipline to pray. It takes discipline to make time to read Scripture. It is a discipline to attend and participate in public worship. And it is a discipline to tithe, a good step in arriving at a practical discipline in all financial matters, including living within a budget.

Giving money is somewhat like saving money. Few people are able to save very much money unless they discipline themselves to set aside a certain amount or percentage of their income, first. So it is with tithing.

Finally, each individual must test tithing in the laboratory of personal experience. No man can render a verdict—a valid verdict, that is—on tithing until he has tried it.

Evangelical Christianity declares and asks, "God has acted for you; what is your response?" A reasonable first step is to acknowledge the Lordship of Jesus Christ by giving on a proportionate basis, by setting aside that proportion first, and as a self-discipline, to give a tithe as a minimum proportion.

XIV

The Ministry of Christian Giving

If giving is to avoid both the legalism of calculated percentages and the contractual concept of the steward and his employer, it must be lifted to its rightful place in the total evangelistic task of the church. All disciplines that deal with percentages will fail to provide joy and satisfaction in giving, unless the giver sees his role in carrying out the commission of our Lord. This commission is very clear, whether it be read from Matthew, Mark, or Luke, or whether it be expressed by Paul. It is "Go . . . preach . . . baptize . . . teach." [1]

The church has been organized to carry out this commission, and, being organized as it is, financial support cannot be separated from the evangelistic task. Evangelism and stewardship are related, closely. Each strengthens the other. The ministry of Christian giving is an integral part of the ministry of evangelism in the church today.

The Gospel Imperative

The moment one receives eternal life through Christ, he is under the imperative to tell others of Christ's love. If you have it, you will want others to have it; if you care not whether others have it, you can be quite certain that you do not have it yourself.

This assumption is implied in the following declaration of the

General Assembly of the Presbyterian Church, U.S.A. in the year 1847:

> The Presbyterian Church is a missionary society, the object of which is to aid in the conversion of the world, and every member of this church is a member for life of said society and bound to do all in his power for the accomplishment of this object.[2]

The following year, the General Assembly emphasized the missionary task of the church by stating:

> Let us never forget that the church was intended to be a missionary society, that we are called into the Kingdom of God to be employed in active efforts to propagate that Kingdom. . . .[3]

These declarations never have been rescinded and, as long as the Presbyterian Church is an evangelical church, they cannot be rescinded. In fact, by the very faith and gospel which evangelical churches declare, this assumption must be acknowledged if such churches are to be true to the faith.

These statements may sound dogmatic and unbending, but they are necessary, for they express a truth: to become a Christian is to enlist in the evangelistic task of the church.

The Meaning of Money

If financial giving is to have its rightful place in the total evangelistic task of the church, money must be seen for what it is. Too often money has been looked upon as a thing of evil. For instance, due to the abuse in financial matters just prior to the Reformation, some of the reformed churches forbade taking an offering in the church. The offering plates were kept in small shelters just inside the church gate. In the present day, there is still a feeling among many people that money, although desirable, carries a bit of taint because of its inherent nature. On the contrary, the role money is intended to play is a good role. Money, like many other things, can be used for good or evil, but the purpose for which it was created is good.

Likewise, the making of money has been looked upon as a questionable pursuit. But money-making, like money itself, can be and should be good. It is a high calling to make money. In a sermon on money, John Wesley urged the people to earn all they could. He advised against harming their health or exploiting the other person in the process of making money; nevertheless, he put this occupation on a lofty plane. He saw money for what it is.

What, then, is money? To the economist, money is a measure of value. In Christian stewardship, it is also a measure of value. As long as a society or a state regulates the gold, silver, or some other "precious" material which guarantees that money will maintain a certain standard of value, a man can store up his time, talent, and strength in the form of money. When he wishes, he can go to this storehouse and exchange his stored-up value for time, talent, and strength. Money, then, is value in negotiable form. To the hungry, it is food; to one who is ill, it is medicine and health; to one who is without shelter, it is a house.

Money Is You

Since money is stored-up value, it enables the Christian to participate in the evangelistic and missionary task of the church through his giving. When a man gives his money, he is giving a part of himself.

A television program—"You Are There"—takes the viewer to various parts of the world or re-enacts some important event in the past; and, through the medium of television, the viewer is present on the scene. The same thing happens for the Christian through his gifts, for by the use of this receptacle of value, known as money, a Christian can be present in the total witness of the church.

As Lester Zook works to offer the people of Mexico the abundant life by improving the land through contour farming, irrigation, strip cropping, tree planting, and the introduction of better poultry, *you are there*. When Alice Strangway captures the devils which cause rickets, pellagra, anemia, goiter, scurvy, and diarrhea and places them in a test tube (which is the beginning of their being driven out) *you are there*. When that diesel pump provides water for the withering crops in Valdala, India, and Gifford Towle assures the people their children will not starve, *you are there*.[4] When the missionaries of your denomination present the gospel and invite the people in faraway places to enter into eternal life through Christ, *you are there*.

Through the ministry of giving, every Christian can respond to the needs of the world as did Isaiah. He saw a need, and to see a need is to hear a call. Isaiah answered that call by saying, "Here am I; send me." [5] Each of us can answer with these same words because of the nature of our money. We are in our money, for it is part of us that has been stored up in negotiable form. Each of us can say, "Here am I, Lord, in my money; send me."

This is the thought expressed by the late Bishop Francis McConnell when he said: "The giver comes nearest giving himself when he gives money—gives, that is, till he himself knows that he is giving." [6] Represented in every American coin and negotiable note is a little of the gold that is stored at Fort Knox, Kentucky. Likewise, in every coin and note which comes into our hands in exchange for our time, talent, or strength, there is a little of ourselves. Seen in this light, the words of Lowell take on a deeper meaning: "The gift without the giver is bare." [7] In fact, if a man has made his money by toil and talent, it is impossible for him to give money without giving himself. Henry B. Trimble says, "Money as a form of power is so intimately related to the possessor that one cannot consistently give money without giving self, nor can one give self without giving money." [8]

In 1949-1950 one denomination—the Church of God—captured the imagination of its members by figuring how much money was required to carry the missionary program of the denomination for each minute, hour, day, and week. In making his commitment to the missionary program, each member underwrote the total program for a certain period of time. It took $120 to carry the program for one hour, and some people underwrote an hour or more. This is an illustration of the dramatic way in which people can be shown how they are present in their giving.

In 1952, L. L. Gwaltney estimated it took $20 per minute to support all the missionary educational benevolent work in an average state in the Southern Baptist Convention. He tells of a doctor who gave through the Co-operative Program each week the amount he receives for one house visit. In doing so, this doctor supported all the mission work done by his state for 23 minutes. A stenographer supported the work for 4 minutes by giving an hour of her earnings each week. A farmer each week gave the earnings from two dairy cows, and his gift carried the work for 10 minutes. One can hardly doubt the claim that interest in the work of the church is much greater when the Co-operative Program is made personal in terms like these.[9]

All this is not to imply that one can substitute a material gift for his time and talents in the church. Instead, a portion of one's time, talent, and money should be dedicated specifically to the work of Christ and his church. The man who is giving full-time work in the ministry will want to be faithful in giving a portion of his income. Likewise, the man whose time and talents may be worth millions of dollars cannot substitute rightly his money for time and talents in Christian work.

A telling illustration of this took place in the ministry of the late John Timothy Stone. While he was pastor of the Fourth Presbyterian Church in Chicago, Dr. Stone saw the need of organizing an "Invitation Committee" to do personal evangelism.

He asked a consecrated layman to be chairman—a man who was a merchant prince, the president of a great organization and trust—who declined because he felt he was too busy. However, he assured Dr. Stone that he would underwrite the financial cost of this program. Dr. Stone told the man the Lord needed him— the man—not his money. The layman then consented to be chairman, leading his committee and church in the work of evangelism.[10] Money cannot be substituted for one's time and talent, and time and talent cannot be substituted for one's money. We are to be faithful stewards of all that has been entrusted to us. Nevertheless—whether it be money, time, or talent—when a man gives, he gives a part of himself.

Evangelists All

Rising out of a distorted concept of Christian devotion, there grew up in the Medieval Church the idea of a double standard— one for the clergy and another for the laity. Out of this there also developed the idea that the clergy and laity were in two entirely different categories. In fact, in Roman Catholic doctrine the "church" is made up of the "clergy."

Protestantism, mistakenly, has allowed a double standard of function to develop which has militated against Christian giving and the total evangelistic task of the church. Too often the minister has been looked upon as the one who is to make financial sacrifices for the causes of Christ. Frequently, in supporting the pastor, the people have looked upon him as one who should have little of this world's goods because of his calling. The story is told of one layman who defended this position with the assumption that a minister was to have "souls for his hire." Whenever an increase was proposed in the pastor's salary, this layman would object, noting that he should have "souls for his hire." Alas, the pastor heard this once too often and replied, "But a man can't eat souls . . . and even if he could, it would take a dozen like yours to make a square meal."

Asbury's assumption that poverty among the preachers was a guarantee they would remain humble and spiritual, was a welcome word to many laymen, and they responded by praying, "God, you keep them humble, and we'll keep them poor."

Actually, some people have looked upon their minister as a case of charity. Their motive for giving was to take care of a man and his family, rather than being motivated by an evangelistic concern. The doctrine of the priesthood of believers has emphasized the freedom with which each individual can approach the throne of grace, but it has been neglected in making clear the responsibility of each individual to bring others to the throne of grace also.

In his letter to the Christians in Rome, Paul raises a series of questions which cannot be answered adequately in our day apart from the ministry of Christian giving. He asks, "How shall people confess Christ if they do not believe; and how shall they believe if they have not heard; and how shall they hear without preachers; and how shall they preach, except they be sent?" [11] Christian giving is the answer to the final question as to the means by which those who are called to preach are to be sent to preach.

At the beginning of this chapter the assumption was expressed that the moment a man enters the Christian life, he thereby commits himself to some role in the evangelistic task. In these concluding lines, the reader's attention is called to the words of Paul and Peter, who speak of the Christian's stewardship in terms of the gospel which has been entrusted to us.

Paul was speaking to ministers or apostles when he spoke of being stewards of the mysteries of God.[12] However, the very nature of the gospel places this treasure in the hands of every believer. Therefore, whether layman or minister, Paul's words are to be heeded. Or, consider the words of I Peter 4:10, "As every man hath received the gift, even so minister the same one to another, as good stewards of the manifold grace of God." Again, each Christian, minister or layman, is a trustee of God's manifold grace in Christ.

A man may decide either to accept or to reject Jesus Christ. But, once he has accepted Christ, it is not for him to decide whether or not he will be a steward, for he becomes a steward when he becomes a Christian. He may be a good steward or he may be a poor steward; nevertheless, he *is* a steward. He has been entrusted with the gospel of Jesus Christ and has been given the gift of eternal life, and it is his high calling to share this gift with others. The one requirement that is placed on a steward is that he be found faithful.[13] The ministry of Christian giving is fulfilled to the extent that a man is faithful in the stewardship of the gospel and of all that is his to share.

Notes by Chapters

Notes to Chapter I

1. Acts 2:45.
2. Acts 6:1-6.
3. I Cor. 16:1-2.
4. I Cor. 16:3; II Cor. 8:19; Acts 20:4.
5. Matt. 10:10.
6. I Cor. 9:6-11.
7. Revised Standard Version of I Cor. 9:14—"In the same way, the Lord commanded that those who proclaim the gospel should get their living by the gospel."
8. I Tim. 5:17.
9. Philippians 4:14-18.
10. II Cor. 11:8.
11. II Cor. 8:9.
12. Helen B. Harris, trans., *Apology of Aristides* (London: Hodder and Stoughton, 1891), p. 108.
13. Justin Martyr and Athenagoras, *The Writings of Justin Martyr and Athenagoras,* Marcus Dods and George Reith, trans. (Alexander Roberts and James Donaldson, eds., *Ante-Nicene Christian Library,* II: Edinburgh: T. and T. Clark, 1868), 65-66.
14. Quintus Sept. Flor. Tertullianus, *The Writings of Quintus Sept. Flor. Tertullianus,* S. Thelwall and Dr. Holmes, trans., I (Alexander Roberts and James Donaldson, eds., *Ante-Nicene Christian Library,* XI; Edinburgh: T. and T. Clark, 1869), 119.
15. *The Teaching of the Twelve Apostles with Illustrations from the Talmud,* two lectures by C. Taylor (Cambridge: Deighton Bell and Co., 1886), p. 134.
16. Irenaeus, *The Writings of Irenaeus,* Alexander Roberts and W. H. Rambaut, trans., (Alexander Roberts and James Donaldson, eds., *Ante-Nicene Christian Library,* V; Edinburgh: T. and T. Clark, 1868), Book IV, chap. XVIII, 433.
17. *The Apostolic Constitutions,* James Donaldson, ed. (Alexander Roberts and James Donaldson, eds., *Ante-Nicene Christian Library,* XVII; Edinburgh: T. and T. Clark, 1870), Book VII, par. 29, 189.

18. Henry Lansdell, *The Sacred Tenth* (2 vols., London: Society for Promoting Christian Knowledge, 1906), I, 182-183.

19. Luke 18:12.

20. Matt. 23:23.

21. Acts 11:29.

22. I Cor. 16:1-2.

23. Irenaeus, *op. cit.,* Chap. XIII, 414.

24. Irenaeus, *op. cit.,* Vol. I, pp. 484-485.

25. *The Ante-Nicene, Nicene, and Post-Nicene Fathers,* VII, 413.

26. *The Ante-Nicene, Nicene, and Post-Nicene Fathers,* V, 429.

27. Joseph Bingham, *Originas Ecclesiasticas* or *Antiquities of the Christian Church* (8 vols., London: Printed for William Straker, 1834), I, 468-469.

28. Eusebius of Caesarea, *The Ecclesiastical History and the Martyrs of Palestine,* Hugh Jackson Lawler and John Ernest Leonard Oulton, trans. (2 vols., London: Society for Promoting Christian Knowledge, 1927), I, 293-294.

Notes to Chapter II

1. Joseph Cullen Ayer, *A Source Book for Ancient Church History* (New York: Charles Scribner's Sons, 1913), p. 283.

2. Edward William Scudamore, "Oblations," *A Dictionary of Christian Antiquities,* William Smith and Samuel Cheetham, eds. (2 vols., Hartford: J. B. Burr Publishing Co., 1880), II, 1420.

3. St. Jerome, *Letters and Select Works,* Philip Schaff and Henry Wace, trans. (*Nicene and Post-Nicene Fathers,* VI; New York: The Christian Literature Company, 1893), p. 91.

4. Smith and Cheetham, eds., *A Dictionary of Christian Antiquities, op. cit.,* II, 1864.

5. Smith and Cheetham, *op. cit.*

6. Smith and Cheetham, *op. cit.*

7. Smith and Cheetham, *op. cit.*

8. *Nicene and Post-Nicene Fathers,* First Series, VIII, 668.

9. Quoted by various authors, *viz:* Smith and Cheetham, *op. cit.,* II, 1864.

10. Morris Fuller, *Our Title Deeds* (London: Griffith, Farran, Okeden, and Welsh, 1890), p. 39.

11. *Nicene and Post-Nicene Fathers, op. cit.,* X, 395-396.

12. *Ibid.,* p. 441.

13. John Seldon, *The Historie of Tithes* (Written from the *Inner Temple,* April 4, 1618), pp. 169-170.

14. Fuller, *op. cit.,* p. 41.

15. Fuller, *op cit.,* pp. 41-42.

16. *Ibid.,* p. 42.

17. Ayer, *op. cit.,* p. 531.

Notes to Chapter III

1. Williston Walker, *A History of the Christian Church* (New York: Charles Scribner's Sons, 1945), p. 191.

2. *Loc. cit.*

3. William E. Lunt, *Papal Revenues in the Middle Ages* (New York: Columbia University Press, 1934), II, pp. 201-202.

4. *Ibid.,* I, 63.

5. *Ibid.,* II, 45-48.

6. Henry Thomas Armfield, "Vacancy," *A Dictionary of Christian Antiquities,* William Smith and Samuel Cheetham, eds. (Hartford: J. B. Burr Publishing Co., 1880), II, p. 2009.

7. *Loc. cit.*

8. André Lagarde, *The Latin Church in the Middle Ages,* Archibald Alexander, trans. (New York: Charles Scribner's Sons, 1915), p. 331.

9. W. E. Lunt, "The First Levy of Papal Annates," *The American Historical Review,* 18:50-51, October, 1912.

10. Lagarde, *op. cit.,* p. 312.

11. Henry Gee and William J. Hardy, *Documents Illustrative of English Church History* (London: Macmillan and Co., Ltd., 1896), p. 148.

12. *Ibid.,* pp. 178-181.

13. Lunt, *Papal Revenues in the Middle Ages, op. cit.,* II, 381.

14. *Loc. cit.*

15. *Ibid.,* I, 381-382.

16. Lagarde, *op. cit.,* p. 325.

17. *Ibid.,* p. 327.

18. *Ibid.,* pp. 327-328.

19. *Ibid.,* p. 328.

20. Robert Sinker, "Pallium," *A Dictionary of Christian Antiquities, op. cit.,* II, 1547-1548.

21. *Ibid.,* 1548.

22. Lagarde, *op. cit.,* p. 329.

23. "Infallible Indulgences," *All the Year Round,* 23:367, March 19, 1870.

24. Joseph Bingham, *Originas Ecclesiasticas* or *Antiquities of the Christian Church* (8 vols.,, London: Printed for William Straker, 1834), I, 569.

25. *Ibid.,* 570-571.

26. Samuel Cheetham, "Pluralities," *A Dictionary of Christian Antiquities, op. cit.,* II, 1646.

27. Oscar Albert Marti, *Economic Causes of the Reformation in England* (New York: The Macmillan Company, 1929), p. 157.

28. Lagarde, *op. cit.,* p. 305.

29. Lunt, *Papal Revenues in the Middle Ages, op. cit.,* II, 55.

30. *Loc. cit.*

31. Lagarde, *op. cit.,* p. 306.

32. Marti, *op. cit.,* p. 58.

33. Lagarde, *op. cit.*, p. 320.
34. *Ibid.*, p. 321.
35. Lunt, *Papal Revenues in the Middle Ages, op. cit.*, II, 82-86.
36. Lagarde, *op. cit.*, pp. 308-309.
37. *Ibid.*, p. 311.
38. *Ibid.*, I, 110.
39. Lunt, *Papal Revenues in the Middle Ages, op. cit.*, II, 302.
40. *Ibid.*, II, 308.
41. Gee and Hardy, *op. cit.*, p. 148.
42. Simon Fish, "The Supplication of Beggars," *The Harleian Miscellany* (London: Printed for John White and others, n.d.), II, p. 542.
43. *Loc. cit.*
44. *Ibid.*, p. 149.
45. *Ibid.*, p. 218.
46. Gee and Hardy, *op. cit.*, p. 148.
47. Henry Charles Lea, "The Eve of the Reformation," *Cambridge Modern History*, A. W. Ward and others, eds. (New York: The Macmillan Company, 1903), I, Chap. XIX, 670.
48. Lunt, *Papal Revenues in the Middle Ages, op. cit.*, I, 135.
49. Lea, *op. cit.*, I, 670.
50. Lunt, *Papal Revenues in the Middle Ages, op. cit.*, I, 135.
51. Lea, *op. cit.*, I, 670.
52. Lunt, *Papal Revenues in the Middle Ages, op. cit.*, II, 537.
53. Thomas M. Lindsay, *A History of the Reformation* (New York: Charles Scribner's Sons, 1906), I, 15.

Notes to Chapter IV

1. Thomas Aquinas, *The Summa Theologia* (London: Burns, Oates, and Washbourne, Ltd., 1914), VI, pt. II, ques. 5, art. 7, 82.
2. C. Anderson Scott, *Romanism and the Gospel* (Philadelphia: The Westminster Press, 1937), p. 27.
3. Philip Schaff, ed., *A Select Library of the Nicene and Post-Nicene Fathers* (First Series, New York: The Christian Literature Company, 1890), II, p. 520.
4. *Ibid.*, II, 208.
5. *Ibid.*, I, 73.
6. Thomas M. Lindsay, *A History of the Reformation* (New York: Charles Scribner's Sons, 1906), I, 218-219.
7. Thomas Aquinas, *op. cit.*, XVIII, ques. 13, art. 2, 213-215.
8. *Ibid.*, XVIII, ques. 25, art. 1, 309.
9. Lindsay, *op. cit.*, chapter on "Indulgences," I, 216-260.
10. William E. Lunt, *Papal Revenues in the Middle Ages* (New York: Columbia University Press, 1934), I, 115-116.
11. Ernest F. Henderson, *Select Historical Documents* (London: George Bell and Sons, 1892), p. 343.
12. *Ibid.*, p. 350.

13. "Infallible Indulgences," *All the Year Round,* 23:366, March 19, 1870.

14. "Roman Sheep-Shearing," *All the Year Round,* 3:431, August 11, 1860.

15. B. J. Kidd, *Documents Illustrative of the Continental Reformation* (Oxford: At the Clarendon Press, 1911), p. 3.

16. The amount is stated by various authors from 20,000 to 30,000 gulden.

17. Jean H. D'Aubigné, *History of the Reformation of the Sixteenth Century* (London: Religious Tract Society, 1846), I, p. 242.

18. D'Aubigné, *op. cit.*

19. J. Donovan, trans., *The Catechism of the Council of Trent* (New York: Catholic School Book Company), p. 248.

20. Herbert Thurston, "Relics," *The Catholic Encyclopedia* (New York: Robert Appleton Company, 1911), XII, 735.

21. Lindsay, *op. cit.,* I, 131.

22. Thurston, *op. cit.,* p. 737.

23. "Roman Sheep-Shearing," *op. cit.,* p. 492.

24. *Ibid.,* III, 104-105. Coulton estimates that one must multiply the figures in the early fourteenth century by about forty and by at least twenty-five or thirty in 1500, to get the equivalent in modern values.

25. "Infallible Relics," *All the Year Round,* 23:353, March 12, 1870.

26. Thurston, "Relics," *op. cit.,* XII, 737.

27. André Lagarde, *The Latin Church in the Middle Ages,* Archibald Alexander, trans. (New York: Charles Scribner's Sons, 1915), pp. 337-338.

28. *Ibid.,* p. 337.

29. Charles Edward Smith, *Papal Enforcement of Some Medieval Marriage Laws* (University, La.: Louisiana State University Press, 1940), p. 195.

Notes to Chapter V

1. Chapter II.

2. Simon Degge, *The Parsons Counsellor* (London: Printed by the Assigns of Richard and Edward Atkins, Esquires, 1677), 448 pp.

3. Degge, *op. cit.*

4. Degge, *op. cit.*

5. Degge, *op. cit.*

6. *Ibid.,* p. 220.

7. *Loc. cit.*

8. *Loc. cit.*

9. Degge, p. 265.

10. *Ibid.,* p. 266.

11. *Ibid.,* p. 279.

12. *Ibid.,* p. 300.

13. *Ibid.,* p. 231.

14. *Ibid.*, p. 255.

15. *Ibid.*, p. 237.

16. *Ibid.*, p. 324.

17. *Ibid.*, p. 246.

18. *Ibid.*, pp. 246-247.

19. *Ibid.*, p. 263.

20. *Ibid.*, p. 259.

21. R. R. Naftel, "Tithe Battles," *The Hibbert Journal,* 32:256, October, 1933-July, 1934.

22. B. J. Kidd, *Documents Illustrative of the Continental Reformation* (Oxford: At the Clarendon Press, 1911), pp. 175-176.

23. Thomas M. Lindsay, *A History of the Reformation* (New York: Charles Scribner's Sons, 1906), II, 31.

24. R. R. Naftel, *op. cit.*, pp. 255-257.

25. Degge, *op. cit.*, p. 324.

26. Naftel, *op. cit.*, p. 256.

27. *Loc. cit.*

28. Degge, *op. cit.*, p. 251.

29. Richard Bartram, "Tithes, Ordinary and Extraordinary," *The British Quarterly Review,* 82:63-77, July, 1885.

30. "Revolt of British Farmers Against the Tithe," *The Literary Digest,* 116:15, September 23, 1933.

31. *Loc. cit.*

32. "The Proposal About Tithe," *The Spectator,* 59:1333, October 9, 1886.

33. "Prosecutions of Quakers, and the Original of Tythes," *The Gentleman's Magazine,* 7:154-56, March, 1737.

34. "Some Considerations Touching the Payment of Tythes," *The Gentleman's Magazine,* 7:131-34, March, 1737.

35. "Thoughts Concerning Tythes," *Blackwood's Edinburgh Magazine* 3:148-151, May, 1818.

36. "The Revolt of the Clergy," *The Contemporary Review,* 75:323-327, March, 1899.

37. "The Unpopular Tithe," *The Saturday Review,* 157:592, May 26, 1934.

38. Willoughby Dewar, "Church Taxes or Tithe?" *The Saturday Review,* 152:780, December 19, 1931.

39. Lord Stanley, "The Church Rate Question Considered," *Edinburgh Review,* 109:35, January, 1859.

40. "The English Church-Rates, and the Scotch Church Establishment," *Blackwood's Edinburgh Magazine,* 51:683, May, 1837.

41. Stanley, *op. cit.*, p. 35.

42. *Ibid.*, p. 37.

43. "The English Church-Rate, and the Scotch Church Establishment," *op. cit.*, p. 686.

44. Stanley, *op. cit.*, p. 37.

45. *Loc. cit.*

46. Stanley, *op. cit.*, pp. 34-35.

47. Mary Aldis, "Reminiscences of a Church-Rate Struggle," *The Contemporary Review*, 57:424-425, March, 1890.

48. Stanley, *op. cit.*, p. 37.

49. *Ibid.*, p. 38.

50. *Loc. cit.*

51. Ernst Troeltsch, *The Social Teaching of the Christian Churches*, Olive Wyon, trans. (London: George Allen and Unwin Ltd., 1931), II, 487.

52. Lindsay, *op. cit.*, I, 410.

53. *Ibid.*, I, 69-70.

54. George Park Fisher, *The Reformation* (New York: Charles Scribner's Sons, 1906), p. 153.

Notes to Chapter VI

1. Charles F. Dole, "The Voluntary System in the Support of Churches," *The Unitarian Review*, 28:22, July, 1887.

2. *Op. cit.*

3. *Ibid.*, p. 23.

4. Williston Walker, *A History of Congregational Churches in the United States* (New York: The Christian Literature Co., 1894), p. 231.

5. Sanford H. Cobb, *The Rise of Religious Liberty in America* (New York: The Macmillian Company, 1902), p. 64.

6. Anson Phelps Stokes, *Church and State in the United States* (New York: Harper & Brothers, 1950), I, 116. ,

7. Dole, *op cit.*, p. 23, and Walker, *op. cit.*, p. 74.

8. John Waddington, *Congregational History*, 1567-1700 (2nd ed.; London: Longmans, Green, and Co., 1880), p. 420.

9. Dole, *op. cit.*, p. 24.

10. Waddington, *op. cit.*, p. 240.

11. Dole, *op. cit.*, p. 24.

12. Robert F. Lawrence, *The New Hampshire Churches* (Published for the author: By the Claremont Manufacturing Company, 1856), p. 478.

13. John Wesley, *Sermons on Several Occasions* (New York: O. Scott, 1846), I, 475-483.

14. *Ibid.*, I, 481.

15. *Ibid.*, I, 484-493.

16. John Telford, ed., *The Letters of John Wesley* (London: The Epworth Press, 1931), VI, p. 130.

17. Wesley, *op. cit.*, II, 280-288.

18. *Ibid.*, II, 283.

19. *Ibid.*, II, 287.

20. *Ibid.*, II, 429-435.

21. *Ibid.*, II, 528-533.

22. *Ibid.*, II, 530.

23. Minutes, I, 6.

24. William Warren Sweet, *The Rise of Methodism in the West* (New York: The Methodist Book Concern, 1920), p. 48.

25. Robert Emory, *History of the Discipline of the Methodist Episcopal Church* (New York: Lane and Scott, 1851), p. 42.

26. Minutes, I, 28-29.

27. Emory, *op. cit.*, p. 237.

28. Minutes, I, 39.

29. Emory, *op. cit.*, pp. 237-238.

30. Abel Stevens, *History of the Methodist Episcopal Church in the United States of America* (New York: Carlton and Porter, 1866-1867), III, p. 19.

31. Emory, *op. cit.*, p. 238.

32. *Ibid.*, p. 11.

33. As early as June 8, 1780, Asbury recorded in his *Journal* a concern over the frequent location of married men: "We spoke of a plan for building houses in every circuit for preachers' wives, and the society to supply their families with bread and meat...." Ezra Squire Tipple, ed., *The Heart of Asbury's Journal* (New York: Eaton and Mains, 1904), p. 173.

34. James Youngs, *A History of the Most Interesting Events in the Rise and Progress of Methodism in Europe and America* (New Haven, Conn.: A. Daggett and Co., 1830), p. 369.

35. Emory, *op. cit.*, p. 291.

36. Nathan Bangs, *A History of the Methodist Episcopal Church* (New York: T. Mason and G. Lane, pub. Vols. I, II, III, 1838-1840; G. Lane and P. P. Sandford, pub. Vol. IV, 1842), II, p. 363.

37. *Ibid.*, II, 357.

38. G. W. Musgrave, *The Polity of the Methodist Episcopal Church in the United States: Being an Exposure* (Baltimore: Printed by Richard J. Matchett, 1843), p. 163.

39. William Annan, *The Difficulties of Arminian Methodism* (Philadelphia: William S. and Alfred Martien, 1860), p. 290.

40. The year of 1844 was selected because for the first time all but three of the 34 annual conferences reported ministers' salaries.

41. Harvey Reeves Calkins, *A Man and His Money* (New York: The Methodist Book Concern, 1914), p. 87.

42. Bangs, *op. cit.*, II, 244.

43. *Ibid.*, II, 215-216.

44. *Ibid.*, II, 416.

45. Emory, *op. cit.*, p. 303.

46. Matthew 12 records the action of a poor widow who gave two mites. The term "mite" frequently is applied to a small gift, regardless of the percentage of the total wealth of the giver. Thus the story is distorted.

47. Tipple, *op. cit.*, p. 678.

48. William Warren Sweet, *Religion on the American Frontier—1783-1840: Methodism* (Chicago: The University of Chicago Press, 1946), p. 49, n. 39.

49. *Loc. cit.*

Notes to Chapter VII

1. Henry A. Foote, "The Taxation of Churches," *The Unitarian Review* 7:251-252, April, 1897.

2. Williston Walker, *A History of Congregational Churches in the United States* (New York: The Christian Literature Co., 1894), p. 233.

3. *Loc. cit.*

4. *Ibid.*, pp. 233-234.

5. Thomas Jefferson Wertenbaker, *The Puritan Oligarchy* (New York: Charles Scribner's Sons, 1947), p. 65.

6. George Woodruff Winans, *First Presbyterian Church of Jamaica, New York* (Jamaica: Published by the church, 1943), p. 9.

7. *Ibid.*, p. 11.

8. *Ibid.*, p. 44.

9. Jonathan F. Stearns, *Historical Discourses, Relating to the First Presbyterian Church in Newark* (Newark: Printed at the *Daily Advertiser* Office, 1853), p. 14.

10. *Ibid.*, p. 89, n. 1.

11. *Ibid.*, p. 96, n. 2.

12. *Ibid.*, p. 102, n. 2.

13. Walker, *op cit.*, pp. 234-235.

14. Wertenbaker, *op. cit.*, p. 295.

15. *Ibid.*, I, 49-68, gives the complete letter. Other writers, especially E. T. Corwin and others, *A History of the Reformed Church, Dutch; The Reformed Church, German; and The Moravian Church in the United States* (New York: The Christian Literature Co., 1894) give valuable material on religious life in New Netherland.

16. *Ibid.*, I, 46 and 75.

17. *Ibid.*, I, 425.

18. *Ibid.*, I, 121.

19. *Ibid.*, I, 44-45.

20. *Ibid.*, I, 582 and 584.

21. *Loc. cit.*

22. *Ibid.*, I, 618.

23. *Ibid.*, I, 504.

24. *Ibid.*, I, 664.

25. Anson Phelps Stokes, *Church and State in The United States* (New York: Harper & Brothers, 1950). I, 163. The source given by Stokes and others is Williams Walker Hening, *Statutes at Large*, I, 67-75.

26. Sanford H. Cobb, *The Rise of Religious Liberty in America* (New York: The Macmillan Company, 1902), p. 75.

27. "History of Revivals of Religion," *American Education Society,* 4:122, November, 1831.

28. William Warren Sweet, *Religion on the American Frontier—1783-1840: Methodism* (Chicago: The University of Chicago Press, 1946), p. 30.

29. *Ibid.*, pp. 30-31.

30. Cobb, *op. cit.,* p. 80.

31. *Ibid.,* p. 81.

32. Peter G. Mode, *Source Book and Bibliographical Guide for American Church History* (Menasha, Wisconsin: George Banta Publishing Company, 1921), p. 13, quoted from Hening, *op. cit.,* I, 242-243.

33. Sweet, *op. cit.,* p. 31.

34. This case is mentioned by various authors. Especially interesting is Cobb, *op. cit.,* pp. 108-111.

35. Stokes, *op. cit.,* I, 164.

36. *Loc. cit.*

37. "North Carolina," *The Columbia Encyclopedia,* ed.-in-chief, Clarke F. Ansley, 1935, 20th printing, 1947, p. 1278.

38. *Loc. cit.*

39. Cobb, *op. cit.,* p. 117.

40. *Ibid.,* p. 120.

41. *Ibid.,* pp. 121-122.

42. *Ibid.,* pp. 125-128.

43. *Ibid.,* p. 131.

44. *Ecclesiastical Records of the State of New York,* II, 1045.

45. *Ibid.,* II, 1048.

46. *Ibid.,* II, 1073-1074.

47. *Ibid.,* II, 1077.

48. *Ibid.,* III, 1530.

49. *Ecclesiastical Records of the State of New York,* III, 1595-1596.

50. *Ibid.,* p. 1585.

51. *Ibid.,* III, 1563-1566.

52. *Ibid.,* III, 2015.

53. Ibid., VI, 4316.

54. Benjamin Franklin, *Works,* Vol. 8, p. 506.

Notes to Chapter VIII

1. E. T. Corwin, *History of the Reformed Church,* p. 28. Sebastian Crol and Jan Huyck preceded Michaelius, but they were not ordained ministers; they were called *Kranken-Besoeckers,* or comforters of the sick.

2. *Ecclesiastical Records of New York,* I, 49-68, contain the letter which Michaelius wrote to Adrian Smoutius in Amsterdam.

3. James M. MacDonald, *Two Centuries in the History of the Presbyterian Church, Jamaica, L. I.* (New York: Robert Carter & Brothers, 1862), p. 38.

4. Robert F. Lawrence, *The New Hampshire Churches* (Published for the author: By the Claremont Manufacturing Company, 1856), pp. 435-536.

5. Frank Samuel Child, *The Colonial Parson of New England* (New York: The Baker and Taylor Co., 1896), p. 63.

6. Joseph B. Walker, "Clerical Life in New Hampshire and Hundred Years Ago," *The Congregational Quarterly,* 15:365-383, July, 1873.

7. Lawrence, *op cit.,* pp. 107-108.

8. Ezra Squire Tipple, ed., *The Heart of Asbury's Journal* (New York: Eaton and Mains, 1904), p. 443.

9. Lucy S. Curtiss, *Two Hundred Fifty Years* (Bridgeport: Published by the United Congregational Church, Inc., 1945), p. 26.

10. Richard A. Wheeler, *History of the First Congregational Church, Stonington, Connecticut* (Norwich: T. H. Davis and Company, 1875), p. 42.

11. Lawrence, *op. cit.*, p. 69.

12. *Ibid.*, p. 170.

13. Hamilton Andrews Hill, *History of the Old South Church* (Boston: Houghton Mifflin and Company, 1890), I, 254.

14. E. B. Huntington, *History of Stamford, Connecticut* (Stamford: Published by the author, 1868), p. 235.

15. Wheeler, *op. cit.*, p. 42.

16. Hill, *op. cit.*, I, 429.

17. *Ibid.*, I, 449.

18. William Warren Sweet, *Religion on the American Frontier—1783-1840,* Vol. II, *The Presbyterians* (New York: Harper & Brothers, 1936), p. 548.

19. Hughes Oliphant Gibbons, *A History of Old Pine Street* (Philadelphia: The John C. Winston Company, 1905), p. 26.

20. Conway P. Wing, *A History of the First Presbyterian Church of Carlisle, Pa.* (Carlisle: "Valley Sentinel" Office, 1877), p. 218.

21. Robert Emory, *History of the Discipline of the Methodist Episcopal Church* (New York: Lane and Scott, 1851), p. 229.

22. Bangs, *op. cit.*, III, 50.

23. William Ramsey, *Church Debts: Their Origin, Evils, and Cure* (Philadelphia: Robert E. Peterson, 1851), p. 113.

24. J. Frederick Drippe, *History of the First Presbyterian Church in Germantown* (Philadelphia: Allen, Lane & Scott, 1909), pp. 69-70.

25. "The Passing of Pews for Sale," *The Literary Digest,* 107:22, November 22, 1930.

26. "Free and Unappropriated," *The Spectator,* 76:10, January 4, 1896.

27. "Is Christ in the Rented Pew?" *The Literary Digest,* 48:1051-1052, May 2, 1914.

28. "Pews Free and For Sale," *The Literary Digest,* 60:32, February 8, 1919.

29. *Loc. cit.*

30. Leonard J. Trinterud, *The Forming of an American Tradition* (Philadelphia: The Westminster Press, 1949), p. 68.

31. Shepherd Knapp, *A History of the Brick Presbyterian Church* (New York: Published by the Trustees of the Brick Presbyterian Church, 1909), p. 41.

32. Jonathan F. Stearns, *Historical Discourses, Relating to the First Presbyterian Church in Newark* (Newark: Printed at the Daily Advertiser Office, 1853), p. 129.

33. Knapp, *op. cit.*, pp. 233, 235, and quotations p. 236.

34. Nathan Bangs, *A History of the Methodist Episcopal Church in the*

United States: Being an Exposure (Baltimore: Printed by Richard J. Matchett, 1843), I, 75.

35. *Ibid.,* I, 88.
36. Minutes, I, 2.
37. Emory, *op. cit.,* p. 17.
38. *Ibid.,* p. 19.
39. *Loc. cit.*
40. *Ibid.,* p. 244.
41. *Ibid.,* p. 239.
42. Bangs, *op. cit.,* IV, 175.
43. *Ibid.,* IV, 177.
44. Corwin, *History of the Reformed Church,* p. 34.
45. J. B. Wakeley, *Lost Chapters Recovered from the Early History of American Methodism* (New York: Printed for the author, 1858), p. 69.
46. Bangs, *op. cit.,* II, 264-265.
47. *Ibid.,* II, 296.
48. William Warren Sweet, *Circuit-Rider Days Along the Ohio* (New York: The Methodist Book Concern, 1923), p. 69, n. 16.
49. William Warren Sweet, *Religion on the American Frontier—1783-1830,* Vol. I, *The Baptists* (New York: Henry Holt and Company, 1931), p. 209.
50. *Ibid.,* p. 63, n. 15.
51. *Wilson Papers,* MS (Durrett Collection, University of Chicago), No. 36.
52. Sweet, *Religion on the American Frontier,* Vol. I, *Baptists,* p. 37.
53. *Centenary Souvenir Commemorative of the Completion of a Century by the First Presbyterian Church of Dayton, Ohio* (Dayton: United Brethren Publishing House, 1900), p. 37.
54. Sweet, *Religion on the American Frontier,* Vol. II, *Presbyterians,* p. 510.
55. "Lottery," *The New International Encyclopedia,* Vol. XIV, 2nd ed. (New York: Dodd, Mead and Company, 1915), p. 382.
56. See also John Samuel Ezell, *Fortune's Merry Wheel, The Lottery in America* (Cambridge, Mass.: Harvard University Press, 1959).
57. Eric Bender, *Tickets to Fortune* (New York: Modern Age Books, Inc., 1938), p. 62.
58. *Ibid.,* p. 63.
59. *Ibid.,* pp. 65-66.
60. A. R. Spofford, "Lotteries in American History," *Annual Report of the American Historical Association* (Washington: Government Printing Office, 1893), p. 173.
61. Bender, *op. cit.,* p. 66.
62. *Ibid.,* p. 109.
63. *Ibid.,* p. 111.
64. John Hall, *History of the Presbyterian Church in Trenton, N. J.* (New York: Anson D. F. Randolph, 1859), pp. 105 and 113.
65. Wing, *op. cit.,* p. 71.
66. Gibbons, *op. cit.,* pp. 25-26.

67. Wakeley, *op. cit.,* p. 344. The amount is two pounds, not two hundred pounds. The two zeros refer to shillings and pence.

68. Thomas Holmes Walker, *One Hundred Years of History* (Baltimore: Sun Printing Office, 1902), pp. 30-31.

69. William Reynolds, *A Brief History of the First Presbyterian Church of Baltimore* (Baltimore: Waverly Press, 1913), p. 4.

70. *Ibid.,* p. 6.

Notes to Chapter IX

1. "Beano," *Time,* 26:368,38, November 25, 1935.

2. "Bingo Banned," *Time,* 28:26, December 21, 1936.

3. "Catholics and Chance," *Time,* 30:24, December 27, 1937.

4. *Loc. cit.*

5. "Gambling," *Time,* December 12, 1938.

6. "Reformer," *Time,* 33:71-72, April 24, 1939.

7. William Davidson, "Is Bingo Getting Too Big?", *Collier's,* December 10, 1954, p. 36.

8. *Loc. cit.*

9. B. Seebohm Rowntree, *Betting and Gambling* (London: Macmillan and Co., Ltd., 1905), pp. 15-16.

10. See the recently published book by Fred J. Cook, *A Two-Dollar Bet Means Murder* (New York: The Dial Press, 1961).

11. Mackenzie, *op. cit.,* p. 12.

12. Horace C. Levinson, *The Science of Chance* (New York: Rinehart & Company, 1939), pp. 17-26.

13. Theresa H. Wolcott, "All Sorts of Church Fairs," *The Ladies' Home Journal,* 22:23, November, 1905.

14. William Bayard Hale, "A Study of Church Entertainments," *The Forum,* 20:570. The quotation is taken from Shakespeare's "Two Gentlemen of Verona."

15. *Loc. cit.*

16. Hale, "A Study of Church Entertainments," *op. cit.,* p. 573.

17. "When the Ladies' Aid Needs Money," *The Ladies' Home Journal,* 26:38, September, 1909.

18. Clemence Haskin, "An Army Travels on Its Belly," *The American Mercury,* 27:170 (complete article, pp. 170-176), October, 1932.

19. "Bread on the Waters," *Newsweek,* 11:31, January 23, 1939.

20. "We Want to Raise Some Money for the Church," *The Ladies' Home Journal,* 30:34, September, 1913.

21. C. W. Ferguson, "Goodwin Tries to Save the Church," *Harper's Monthly,* 169:25, June, 1934.

22. *Church and State,* May, 1955, Vol. 8, No. 5, p. 7, and June, 1955, Vol. 8, No. 6, p. 8.

23. Ralph A. Felton, *The Lord's Acre* (Madison, New Jersey: published by the author, 1946), p. 9.

24. John Clarkson, "A $2,500,000 Church Building That Will Pay for Itself," *The American Magazine,* 99:58, January, 1925.

Notes to Chapter XI

1. Proverbs 23:7.

2. Matthew 10:26.

3. Ephesians 2:8,9.

4. George Pitt-Rivers, "The Revolt Against Tithes," *The Nineteenth Century,* 115:311-23, March, 1934.

5. II Corinthians 9:7 (Weymouth Translation).

6. Matthew 6:1-4.

7. Thomas Kane, "A Tithing Autobiography" (Pamphlet No. 8, The Layman Co., 730 Rush Street, Chicago, Illinois, n.d.), p. 3.

8. Thomas Kane, "Does Tithing Pay?" (a tract published by The Layman Co., 730 Rush Street, Chicago, Illinois, n.d.).

9. Gordon B. Hinckley, *What of the Mormons?* (Published by the Church of Jesus Christ of Latter-Day Saints, 1947, address not given), pp. 213-214.

10. See especially P. W. Thompson, *The Whole Tithe* (New York: Marshall Brothers, Ltd., 1924), pp. 146-147.

11. Among other sources, "The Rewards from Tithing," *The Literary Digest,* 82:36-37, August 2, 1924.

12. William G. Shepherd, "Men Who Tithe," *The World's Work,* 48:259-267, July, 1924.

13. "Tithing in Hard Times" (a tract published by The Layman Co., 730 Rush Street, Chicago, Illinois, n.d.).

14. Monroe E. Dodd, *Concerning the Collection* (New York: Fleming H. Revell Company, 1929), pp. 11-12.

15. Raymond Jeffreys, *God Is My Landlord.* (Chicago: Van Kampen Press, 1947), p. 141.

16. *Ibid.,* p. 141.

17. "Tithing in Hard Times" (a tract published by the Layman Co., 730 Rush Street, Chicago, Illinois. n.d.).

18. "Farming for the Lord," *The Literary Digest,* 83:34-35.

19. *Ibid.,* p. 35.

20. "God's Cranberries," *The Literary Digest,* 87:31-32, October 24, 1925.

21. Raymond J. Jeffreys, *God Is My Landlord* (Chicago: Van Kampen Press, 1947), 158 pp.

22. *Ibid.,* p. 31.

23. Genesis 28:22.

24. "Plan for Propagating the Gospel Among the Indians in North America," *The Gentleman's Magazine,* 42:404, September, 1772.

25. "The Church as a Business Investment," *Current Literature,* 41:671-672, December, 1906.

26. "Are Foreign Missions Worth the Cost?" *Current Literature,* 48:522, May, 1910.

27. *Loc. cit.*

28. Frederick Simpich, "How Missionaries Help Foreign Trade," *The Saturday Evening Post,* 196:7, September 8, 1923.

29. *Ibid.,* pp. 114, 117.

30. Henry P. Van Dusen, *They Found the Church There* (New York: Charles Scribner's Sons, 1945).

31. *Ibid.,* p. 2.

32. Anders Nygren, *Agape and Eros,* A. G. Herbert, trans., in three volumes (London: Society for Promoting Christian Knowledge, 1932), 705 pp.

33. Job 1:9.

34. II Corinthians 8:9.

35. II Corinthians 9:7.

Notes to Chapter XII

1. Genesis 43:19, 44:1-4; I Chronicles 28:1; Matthew 20:8; Luke 12:42; 16:1-8.

2. Harvey Reeves Calkins, *A Man and His Money* (New York: The Methodist Book Concern, 1914), p. 109.

3. S. D. Clark, *The Faithful Steward* (New York: Published by M. W. Dodd, 1850), 140 pp.

4. Parsons Cooke, *The Divine Law of Beneficence* (New York: American Tract Society, n.d.), 169 pp.

5. D. X. Junkin, *The Good Steward* (Philadelphia: Presbyterian Board of Publication, 1864), 115 pp.

6. Henry Constable and others, *Gold and the Gospel* (London: James Nisbet and Co., 1853), 439 pp.

7. Samuel B. Copen, "Four Years of the Laymen's Movement," *The Missionary Review of the World,* 34:371-378, May, 1911.

8. "The Root of the Matter," *The Prophetic Word,* May, 1951, p. 284.

9. "Christian Ministers Not Beggars," *American Education Society Quarterly Register and Journal,* 8:370-371, May, 1836.

10. Charles F. Beach, *The Muzzled Ox* (Philadelphia: Presbyterian Publication Committee, 1866), 78 pp.

11. "The Gadite, A Challenge to Christian Laymen," *The Independent,* 62:1134-1137, May 16, 1907.

12. "A Minister's Salary," *The Independent,* 62:1381-1387, June 13, 1907.

13. "If the Ministers Went on Strike," *The Literary Digest,* 62:29-30, September 27, 1919.

14. "From Preaching to Plastering," *The Literary Digest,* 79:30-31, December 15, 1923.

Notes to Chapter XIII

1. Henry Lansdell, *The Sacred Tenth* (London: Society for Promoting Christian Knowledge, 1906), I, 1-38.

2. Harvey Reeves Calkins, *A Man and His Money* (New York: The Methodist Book Concern, 1914).

3. "The Peril of the Stewardship Ideal," *The Christian Century,* 43:1414, November 18, 1926.

4. *Ibid., pp.* 1414-1415.

5. J. M. Powis Smith, "The Deuteronomic Tithe," *The American Journal of Theology,* 18:119-126, January, 1914.

6. *The Interpreter's Bible* (New York: Abingdon-Cokesbury Press, 1951), VII, pp. 535-536.

7. Julius King, *Successful Fund-Raising Sermons* (New York: Funk and Wagnalls Company, 1953), p. 259.

Notes to Chapter XIV

1. Matthew 28:19,20; Mark 16:15; Luke 24:46-47; Romans 10:15; Titus 1:3.

2. *Tools for Missionary Education* (Philadelphia: Board of Christian Education of the Presbyterian Church in the U.S.A., 1954), p. 3.

3. *Minutes of the General Assembly of the Presbyterian Church in the U.S.A.* (Philadelphia: Presbyterian Board of Publication, 1948), p. 55.

4. Ralph A. Felton, *Hope Rises from the Land* (New York: Friendship Press, 1955), pp. 3, 27, and 72.

5. Isaiah 6:4.

6. Francis J. McConnell, *Christian Materialism* (New York: Friendship Press, 1936), p. 103.

7. *The Vision of Sir Launfal.*

8. Henry B. Trimble, *The Christian Motive and Method in Stewardship* (New York: Abingdon-Cokesbury Press, 1929 (1946 edition), p. 155.

9. Merrill D. Moore, *Found Faithful* (Nashville: Broadman Press, 1953), pp. 100-101.

10. John Timothy Stone, *Winning Men* (New York: Fleming H. Revell Co., 1946), pp. 53-54.

11. Romans 10:14-15.

12. I Corinthians 4:1.

13. I Corinthians 4:2.